Staying Safe While You Smoke or Grill

Common sense, you say? Maybe, but every year a surprising number of good times around the grill end up scary times around a burn. Following a few tips keeps your cooking on track.

- **Keep your grill, smoker, or chimney starter at least 10 feet away from your house, trees, and anything else that may catch fire.**

- **Avoid loose-fitting clothing.** You don't need to wear young-Travolta-level tight pants, but loose clothing is much more likely to catch fire than fitted clothing.

- **Keep a fire extinguisher within reach, or have a hose at the ready for addressing any accidental or out-of-control fires.**

- **If you plan to cook on a wooden deck, thoroughly wet down the area before you start.**

- **Make sure the young'uns keep their distance.** Delineate the "no-kid zone" by making a chalk line about a 10-foot radius from the grill or smoker.

- **Don't use lighter fluid.** Lighter fluid isn't ideal for barbecue flavor in the first place, and it's downright dangerous if you try to add it to already hot charcoal. It can catch fire, and that fire leads right back to the bottle in your hands.

- **Don't improvise lighter fluid.** The stuff is nasty to begin with, but trying another flammable in its place when you're in a pinch is incredibly dangerous.

- **Be careful with alcohol.** Yes, alcohol and outside cooking are no strangers — in many eyes, they're inseparable — but that delicious whiskey you're sipping is flammable. Keep that in mind.

- **Be good to your grates.** Clean grates don't catch fire. Gunked-up, grease-ified grates do.

A Few Things to Keep in Mind When Buying Meat

Start with good raw material and you're more likely to get a great finished product. Here are some tips for choosing wisely at the butcher counter:

- **More fat means more flavor.** A well-marbled piece of meat is going to fare better on your grill or smoker than a leaner cut. And, especially for slow cooking, the "luxury cuts" like filet are exactly wrong. You want the cuts that come from the working areas of the animal and have more fat stores.

- **Fresher is better.** Poke the meat you're considering (if it's wrapped, that is). You want it to feel firm and to bounce back after you move your finger away. If it doesn't, it's probably been on the shelf for too long.

- **Liquid is a bad sign.** The red juices you see pooling in a package of meat mean that the meat got too warm. It won't taste as good or be as tender as meat that has been properly refrigerated.

For Dummies: Bestselling Book Series for Beginners

Estimating Temperature

The right temperature for the right job is an important part of grilling or smoking. If you find yourself thermometer-less, here's a guide for estimating temperature with your hand: Hold it 5 or 6 inches above the heat source and time how long you can comfortably keep it there.

- 1 to 2 seconds means your charcoal is hotter than 500° — a high grilling heat.

- 3 to 4 seconds and the temperature is 350° to 400° — medium grill heat.

- 6 seconds means you're at smoking temperature — 250° or less.

Three Important Points for Barbecue Cooking

You hear three things over and over again when you talk to experienced barbecue cooks:

- **Be patient.** Give your food preparation and cooking the time they need to make magic, and give yourself time and room to figure out the ins and outs of barbecue cooking.

- **Have fun.** You're not auditioning for a chef gig at La Grenouille — you're cooking for your friends. Lighten up and enjoy it.

- **Be patient.** Seriously. You're going to mess up sometimes, but you *will* get the process down pat. Promise.

BBQ Sauces, Rubs & Marinades

FOR

DUMMIES®

BBQ Sauces, Rubs & Marinades

FOR DUMMIES®

Traci Cumbay with Tom Schneider

WITHDRAWN

Wiley Publishing, Inc.

BBQ Sauces, Rubs & Marinades For Dummies®

Published by
Wiley Publishing, Inc.
111 River St.
Hoboken, NJ 07030-5774
www.wiley.com

WILEY

About the Authors

Traci Cumbay: Traci cooks and eats quite a bit and then writes about the experiences for publications in Indianapolis, Indiana, where she lives with her husband and son.

Tom Schneider: Tom's passion for authentic barbecue arose during his high school days in Oklahoma and burgeoned over 20 years of uncovering traditional barbecue joints while traveling the United States. Tom is primarily a self-taught cook who, for the past decade, has leveraged his commitment to barbecue into award-winning barbecue recipes while competing in sanctioned barbecue competitions and formal barbecue judging. Tom is owner and pit master for Poppi-Q Bar-B-Que, a specialty catering business in the Indianapolis market.

Dedication

For Richard T. Brink, possibly the worst backyard cook ever to hoist a beer near burning charcoal, and dearly missed.

Authors' Acknowledgments

From Traci: Thanks first to Mike Baker, the acquisitions editor at Wiley who about a year ago left a message on my voice mail asking me whether I wanted to write "the coolest book ever."

I'm seriously indebted to the unflappable and insightful Elizabeth Kuball, the editor who kept me in line, kept me calm, and kept making this book better.

And, especially, thanks to all the barbecue cooks who shared their smarts and recipes for this book; to Brandon Hamilton and Anthony Hanslits, the chefs who contributed some excellent and unique touches; and to Rich Allen, who checked my work and gently guided me back when I was off track.

From Tom: I'd like to thank all the purveyors of great barbecue recipes and proven barbecuing techniques who heeded my plea to share some of their very coveted and trusted knowledge. It is with this generosity that we may continue to incubate future barbecue aficionados for years to come.

A special thanks to the Baron of Barbecue, Mr. Paul Kirk, for his significant contribution to our tasty recipes.

Publisher's Acknowledgments

We're proud of this book; please send us your comments through our Dummies online registration form located at www.dummies.com/register/.

Some of the people who helped bring this book to market include the following:

Acquisitions, Editorial, and Media Development

Project Editor: Elizabeth Kuball

Acquisitions Editor: Mike Baker

Copy Editor: Elizabeth Kuball

Editorial Program Coordinator: Erin Calligan Mooney

Technical Editor: Rich Allen

Recipe Tester: Emily Nolan

Senior Editorial Manager: Jennifer Ehrlich

Consumer Editorial Supervisor and Reprint Editor: Carmen Krikorian

Editorial Assistants: Joe Niesen, Leeann Harney, David Lutton

Cover Photos: Front cover, © Food Image Source/Peter Hogg/StockFood; back cover left, © Lew Robertson/StockFood; back cover middle, © Noel/FoodPix/JupiterImages; back cover right, © Klaus Arras-StockFood Munich/StockFood

Cartoons: Rich Tennant (www.the5thwave.com)

Composition Services

Project Coordinator: Lynsey Stanford

Layout and Graphics: Alissa D. Ellet, Stephanie D. Jumper, Ronald Terry, Christine Williams

Special Art: Elizabeth Kurtzman

Proofreaders: Laura Albert, Bonnie Mikkelson

Indexer: Broccoli Information Management

Special Help

Erin Calligan Mooney

Publishing and Editorial for Consumer Dummies

    Diane Graves Steele, Vice President and Publisher, Consumer Dummies

    Joyce Pepple, Acquisitions Director, Consumer Dummies

    Kristin A. Cocks, Product Development Director, Consumer Dummies

    Michael Spring, Vice President and Publisher, Travel

    Kelly Regan, Editorial Director, Travel

Publishing for Technology Dummies

    Andy Cummings, Vice President and Publisher, Dummies Technology/General User

Composition Services

    Gerry Fahey, Vice President of Production Services

    Debbie Stailey, Director of Composition Services

Contents at a Glance

Recipes at a Glance

Appetizers

Barbecue Sauces

Brines

Cold Sides

Dipping Sauces

Dry Rubs

Entrees

Hot Sides

Marinades

Mop Sauces

Relishes

Vegetables

Table of Contents

Introduction

●●

*B*ig talk surrounds barbecue, talk that would have you believe the topic is impenetrable, that you should be content to pick up a rack of ribs at the local rib shack and call it a day.

Nonsense.

Barbecue is like anything: Dig in and get your apron dirty, and you start finding out what you need to know to keep getting better.

For many people, the pursuit of barbecue perfection becomes all-consuming, edging out sleep and sex for brain space. For others, pulling out the smoker to cook chickens on a sunny Saturday is plenty. Both of these camps start out at the same place: square one. This book picks up at exactly that spot. It tells you what you need to know about barbecue cooking and then gives you the recipes to put theory into practice.

Enjoy the ride — and the results.

About This Book

I wrote this book to be an easy-to-use reference. You're welcome to read it from cover to cover, but you don't have to.

As you dig in, you find

- ✔ All the dirt on the equipment and techniques you need to cook real-deal barbecue
- ✔ Tips from championship barbecue cooks and legendary restaurateurs
- ✔ Inspirations for creating your own signature sauces and rubs
- ✔ Recipes for every stage of barbecue, and even for reimagining leftovers

Conventions Used in This Book

As you work with the recipes in this book, remember the following conventions:

- ✔ Spices are dried unless otherwise specified.

- ✔ Flour is all-purpose unless otherwise specified.

- ✔ Sugar is granulated unless otherwise noted.

- ✔ All temperatures are Fahrenheit. (Refer to the appendix for information about converting temperatures to Celsius.)

You also run into the following conventions throughout the text:

- ✔ *Italic* is used for emphasis and to highlight new words or terms that I define.

- ✔ Monofont is used for Web and e-mail addresses.

- ✔ Sidebars, which are shaded boxes of text, consist of information that's interesting but not necessarily critical to your understanding of the topic. I use them to share stories from the barbecue circuit, hints about finding and using ingredients, and whatever else jumped to mind as I wrote.

What You're Not to Read

This book is designed to give you just what you need to get cooking. In some cases, though, I couldn't resist providing a little further information about a topic. Those tidbits show up in one of two ways, either of which is entirely skippable if you find you aren't searingly curious:

- ✔ **Sidebars:** The gray box around blocks of text indicate that you can skip ahead.

- ✔ **Technical Stuff icon:** Any paragraph marked with the Technical Stuff icon may be interesting to you, but it isn't critical to your understanding of barbecue.

Foolish Assumptions

In order to write this book, I had to keep in mind a few notions about who you might be. I assume that you fit into one or more of the following categories:

✔ Someone who's just getting started as an outdoor cook and wants to make the experience as pleasant as possible by following a well-trod path

✔ A beginning cook who wants to expand his skills with some time-tested tips and new recipes

✔ A barbecue enthusiast looking for some of the back story about the dishes she loves to grub

✔ The smart-thinking spouse or friend of a barbecue cook who's giving this book as a gift in hopes of feasting on the fruits of his purchase

How This Book Is Organized

You can easily find what you're looking for in this book, whether it's a rundown of the types of wood you can use in your smoker or a recipe for coleslaw. Here's an outline of this book's organization.

Part I: Centuries of Barbecue Smarts in Four Chapters

A lot of big talk surrounds barbecue cooking, but the bottom line is that anyone can do it. In this part, I give you all the information you need to get started, explaining how the masters of barbecue do what they do and how you, too, can find and use the equipment, techniques, seasonings, and skills that produce fantastic eats.

Part II: Preparation Prevails: Using Rubs and Marinades

An important first step to great-tasting meat, using a rub adds flavor and helps you develop a nice crust on the meat. Similarly, a good soak in a balanced marinade can make a world of difference in your barbecue. This part tells you about how rubs and marinades work, gives you insight into concocting your own rubs and marinades, and provides lots of great recipes.

Part III: The All-Important Sauce Story

Sauce is the big finish of barbecue and often the first thing that hits the tongues of your guests. This part explains how you use various sauces and shows you how to make a spectrum of sauces from regional barbecue standards to exotic concoctions.

Part IV: Entrees and Sides and Then Some

Sides, salads, and salsas complement a great plate of barbecue, and this part provides you inspiration for cooking up memorable dishes to serve with your impressive ribs and brisket, some recipes for dishes that break the barbecue mold, and others that make use of barbecue leftovers.

Part V: The Part of Tens

Full of chapters that give you easily digestible tidbits of information, this part alerts you to common barbecue mistakes and gives you words to cook by. You find ten places to turn when you want more information and ten hot barbecue competitions or festivals where you can taste inspiration.

Icons Used in This Book

For Dummies signature icons are the little round pictures you see in the margins of the book. They're designed to draw your eye to bits of information I really want to drive home. Here's a list of the icons you find in this book and what they mean:

Some points in these pages are so useful that I hope you keep them in mind as you read. I make a big deal out of these ideas with this icon.

The barbecue pros who contributed to this book have ages of wisdom at the ready. When I relay the tidbits that can save you time, money, or sanity, I emphasize them with this icon.

Wherever I point out possible missteps or potentially dangerous practices, I use this icon to highlight the information. May you experience neither burn nor unbalanced sauce.

 If you're the kind of person who thrives on detail or an overachiever always on the lookout for extra credit, information marked by this icon is for you. But you're welcome to skip it; doing so won't affect your understanding of barbecue cooking.

Where to Go from Here

For Dummies books are set up so that you can flip to the section of the book that meets your present needs, and this book is no exception. When I refer to a concept that I cover in greater detail elsewhere in the book, I tell you which chapter to turn to, and I define terms as they arise to enable you to feel at home no matter where you open the book.

Looking for a great marinade? Turn to Part II. Interested in finding out more about the difference between Memphis barbecue sauce and the versions that come out of Kansas City? Chapter 1 gives you the lowdown (and Part III has recipes for sauces from all over). Dive in and get cooking!

Part I
Centuries of
Barbecue Smarts
in Four Chapters

"Jekyll, old man — I think the spices for your
barbecue may be a bit too strong."

In this part . . .

Sure, you can step outside and throw some weenies on the grill, but with just a little preparation and fore-thought, you can create meals full of wow. This part of the book prepares you for barbecue greatness, giving you the scoop on equipment, ingredients, and techniques that help you cook like a pro.

Chapter 1

Faces of Barbecue:
A Pit, a Plateful, a Party

*A*n unmistakable reaction tears through my body when I get barbecue on the brain. Just talking (or reading or even writing) about it incites a bone-deep craving, making my mouth water and my stomach plead.

I know I'm not alone. Barbecue stirs up a visceral reaction everywhere you go, causing cravings that spur enthusiasts to drive all night or get on a train to get their lips around their favorite ribs. The passion that barbecue incites has created deep friendships and broken others when spats over recipes heated to boiling. Ever heard of chicken soup doing that?

Barbecue is a way of cooking, a party, or the food itself — succulent servings of slow-cooked pork shoulder shredded and mixed with sauce or dry-rubbed ribs with a crackling bark full of paprika, cayenne, and cumin. It's food for laid-back Sundays with friends or raucous family gatherings, for baptisms and funerals and anything in between. It's a way of life for the cooks who travel from competition to competition and those who stay put, running generations-old family restaurants. It's no less lifeblood for the devotees who make more-than-weekly trips to a favorite rib joint or for hobbyists who cook their own barbecue at home.

In this chapter, I run through some of the theories about barbecue's origins and fill you in on the very basics of the cooking method that begat the lifestyle.

First, There Was Fire

Before it became the holy grail of barbecue flavor, smoke was good for keeping away the bugs, and the earliest Americans built fires under their meat while they dried it on frames in the sun to preserve it. Turns out the meat tasted better after the smoke wafted into it, and so started the practice of infusing meat with the flavor of smoke.

Believe that? You have no reason not to, and it's at least as plausible as any of the 47 or so other theories about how barbecue came to be.

The mysteries of barbecue extend far beyond the origin of the word. (Does it come from the French for "whiskers to tail"? Is it a description of the frames used for roasting meat over fire in the West Indies? Dunno — and neither does anybody else.)

Smoking for preservation: How wood works wonders

Somewhere, somehow, some long-ago human figured out that drying food over smoke kept it from rotting, at least for a while longer than doing nothing would have. Smoking food worked well enough in pre-refrigeration days, but the reason wasn't pinned down until much later.

Heat sets free a number of organic acids (including acetic acid, or vinegar) from wood. When those acids fly up onto the meat via smoke, they condense on its surface and change the balance of the meat. The result is a surface pH level that's too low for bacteria to be able to make themselves at home.

Wood smoke also is heavy in *phenols* — high-acidity compounds that prolong the period of time before meats turn rancid.

As you may guess, not all the many chemicals in wood smoke are good for human consumption or respiration. Lucky, then, that the low temperatures you use for slow smoking don't release as much of the unhealthy compounds from wood as high heat does. Keeping the meat as far as you can from the wood as it smokes also cuts down on the opportunity for the harmful compounds to get into the meat and, therefore, into you.

In the upcoming sections, I tell you a few things that are known, believed, or completely fabricated about the start and progress of barbecue. In the brazen and lively world of barbecue, lies and half-truths are as good as facts. Sometimes better.

Facts and fibs about barbecue

Some do-it-yourselfers build smokers out of old refrigerators, which is a little ironic: Had refrigeration become a part of everyday living earlier, barbecue might not exist. Without it, people had to pre-serve meat by salting the bejesus out of it or by smoking it, and that smoking process opened the door for the pits and stands and restaurants that do heady business today.

Barbecue first took hold in the American South and used primarily pork because that's what was available. As barbecue moved across the country, urban conditions in Memphis led cooks to focus on ribs, which took less time and space (and consequently, money) to cook.

In Texas, where cows are common as dust, beef brisket became the definition of barbecue. (I tell you about brisket and the other common cuts of meat that are used in barbecue in Chapter 4.) Heavy German influence in the area helped bring sausage into the barbecue norm, and hot links (spicy smoked sausages) grew to be another Texas barbecue trademark.

The best of all the barbecue traditions melded in Kansas City, and restaurants and hobbyists all over the country maintained and modified barbecue practices in search of their particular definition of perfection. Many will tell you they've found it, and most of these "perfect" barbecue concoctions come from wildly different approaches — including serving crackly pig skin in shredded pork sandwiches; dousing ribs with sauce as a final touch while they're still on the heat (or cooking them in nothing but rub); and using mustard-, vinegar-, or tomato-based sauces.

Everyone thinks his own barbecue is the best. Everyone is right.

From pit to pellet smoker

With scarce resources, resourceful settlers dug pits and cooked their food over hot coals — a far cry from the high-tech barbecue rigs that the pros use to mimic the results of those centuries-ago methods.

Barbecue spread westward across the United States, just like everything else, and morphed a bit along the way. (Check out the upcoming section, "Touring the Four All-American Barbecue Regions.")

Holes in the ground gave way to homemade smokers cut from metal barrels. Industrialization brought nicely engineered and executed home charcoal smokers — and later, gas and electric models — into mass production. (Chapter 2 tells you about the current options for barbecue equipment.)

From its simple beginnings, barbecue has become, of all things, a sport, drawing competitors from around the United States to weekend contests where hundreds slave over mobile pits they paid thousands of dollars for in hopes of taking home a trophy, a small check, and big-time bragging rights. What a shock to anyone who just wanted to be able to chew her meat without an overlong struggle.

Touring the Four All-American Barbecue Regions

Great barbecue happens everywhere, but some human yen to codify things begat four regions of barbecue in the United States. Each region has some significance in the story of barbecue, but none is entirely separate from the others. Although the differences among them are a matter for considerable and vehement discussion, the details of the traditions in the various regions have more in common than they don't. But try telling that to a Tennessean turning up his nose at a Carolina-style, vinegar-sauced, shredded pork sandwich with coleslaw on top.

Throughout this book, you find recipes for barbecue from each of the regions (and from elsewhere). The following sections give you some idea about how each area distinguishes itself.

Carolinas

Squealers fared well with little attention in the Carolina climate, and barbecue from this region reflects that. Primarily pork, often shoulder or whole hog, barbecue in the Carolinas most often means sandwiches. Those sandwiches contain chopped pork from pretty much every part of the pig, including the crackly skin.

Pork in North Carolina is dressed with a touch of vinegary sauce in the eastern part of the state, more generously mixed with vinegary tomato sauce in the west.

Order barbecue in South Carolina and you're most likely to find a mustard-based sauce atop your shredded pork. Wherever you go, it's served on chewy white bread.

Memphis

Ribs are the crux of the Memphis barbecue tradition, and many pit masters there serve them *dry* (cooked with a rub but without sauce). But dry isn't the final word on ribs, and sweet, sticky sauce tops a good portion of those you find in Memphis.

Ribs are a product of the move from the country into the cities as farming became mechanized. Because they're small, ribs cook much more quickly, with less fuel, and in much less space than a whole hog. Although ribs popped up quickly in other urban centers like Chicago and St. Louis, they are forever tied up tight with Memphis barbecue.

Texas

Before same-day shipping to mega grocery stores, people cooked what was available, and in Texas, what's available is beef.

Beef brisket is the hallmark of Texas barbecue, which also strays from the Memphis and Carolina styles by including ham and sausage. Ribs make it onto barbecue platters here, too.

Brisket is a tough cut of meat that's a challenge to master. True Texas pit bosses took to the coarse, amply muscled cuts because of the great finished product that slow smoking provides. They usually give it a douse of rub (or just a sprinkle of salt and pepper) before cooking it over mesquite, slice it across the grain, and serve it with a side of smoky sauce and a slice of white bread.

Kansas City

That thick sauce you find in bottles, the one taking up most of the shelf space in grocery stores' barbecue sauce sections — that sauce is the product of Kansas City.

Most everything else in Kansas City started somewhere else. Its spot at the center of the country positioned it to be the melting pot of barbecue styles, where brisket is as common as a rack of pork ribs. One unique local offering is burnt ends, the bits of brisket from the thin edges that cook quicker than the main part and hang tightly to deep, smoky flavor.

Sauce is the end-all, be-all of barbecue in Kansas City, and sauce means heavy on the tomatoes, light on spice, and full of tangy sweetness. (Think KC Masterpiece, the biggest-selling sauce and a product of Kansas City physician Rich Davis.)

Smoke 'Em If You Got Time

The hallmarks of barbecue are smoke flavor and low-and-slow cooking. Despite so many people insisting upon calling what they do on their gas grill "barbecuing," the practices behind barbecuing and grilling are at odds: Grilling means hot-and-fast cooking and barbecue is its opposite.

Barbecue requires patience at just about every step of the process, from adding a dry rub to the meat before you cook it to letting meat sit a spell before you cut into it.

True barbecue is slow

Barbecue cooking may have come about in part as a form of multi-tasking. Carolinians cooked whole hogs over low heat because it was the best way to ensure that every last bit got cooked without ruining any of the faster-cooking parts. Legend says they also did it because doing so enabled the cook to run off and see to other tasks.

Barbecue cooking requires a temperature somewhere around 250 degrees. (Significant argument surrounds the "correct" cooking temperature. Some argue for 300 degrees or so, others for something in the neighborhood of 180 degrees. As long as you keep the temperature from fluctuating, you can cook great barbecue at about any stop along that range.) By contrast, you grill using a fire that's a good 500 degrees.

Barbecue cooking also owes something to poverty. If everybody in the South had been able to afford tender cuts of meat, high-and-fast cooking would've been fine. The need to turn the dregs of a pig into something tender and tasty brought about the slow-cooking technique.

Cooking meat slowly, at low temperatures, is what makes tough meat tender. Slow cooking gives meat's fat time to render and its connective tissue time to break down. Both those processes lead to softer, easier-to-chew, and more delectable cooked meats.

The story behind your pulled pork sandwich may not be entirely appetizing, but the result is the reason people travel hundreds of miles or plan their vacations around their favorite barbecue spots.

True barbecue is smoked

Without smoke, there is no barbecue. *Smoking* means adding seasoned hardwood to a fire so that it heats up and smokes, releasing its flavor into the meat.

The smoke flavor that ends up in your ribs or brisket depends on the wood you use; pecan is going to give a flavor much different from apple, for example.

You add wood usually in the form of chunks or smaller chips that have been chopped and dried for the express purpose of flavoring your barbecue. Then again, you can run around your backyard picking up sticks from under your oak tree and throw those onto the fire.

One of the hallmarks of slow-smoked meat is a pink ring and, in many cases, a pink tinge throughout the meat. The ring around the edges of the meat comes about because of the gasses released from the smoking wood, which react with the muscle tissue to create the color. A pink tinge in deeper areas arises because of the way the proteins within the meat unfold at lower temperatures. Cook at high temperatures, and the meat's color seeps out early, but when the meat creeps up on the temperature required to loosen the pigment, the color has nowhere to go because the other elements of the meat have already settled in and shut themselves off.

In Chapter 2, you can find out everything you need to know about using wood when you cook.

Making the Most of the Meat

You can accomplish a lot in the way of tenderizing and adding smoke flavor to meat by cooking at low temperatures over charcoal and wood. You achieve even better results when you mix up some marinade or a great rub to work a little cayenne or curry into the meat.

Converting barbecue techniques for backyard grilling

This book is about barbecue, and most of the recipes within it come from true barbecue pit masters, but you're cordially invited to do with the information you find here whatever your heart and stomach desire.

If you want to oven-roast a chicken dressed up in one of the rubs you find in Chapter 6, knock yourself out. If you think shrimp would do nicely doused in one of the marinades from Chapter 7 and then plunked on the grill, you might just be onto something. Want to dip french fries in one of the rich, tomatoey sauces from Part III? Please do.

Any cook worth his sea salt is an innovator. Every technique in this book was new at some point, and there's not a reason under the sun why you shouldn't feel free to experiment, as well.

If you want to try cooking true barbecue but aren't interested in investing in another piece of cooking equipment for your backyard, try utilizing your grill as a smoker. It requires no special equipment but aluminum foil, and I show you how to do it in Chapter 2.

In the following sections, I tell you about the three most-used methods for giving zing to any meat you cook.

Seasoning with rubs

A *rub* is a dry marinade that you sprinkle or pat onto meat before you cook it. Rubs can contain just about anything, and they usually include some salt and sugar. You leave them on for a few minutes before you cook or as long as overnight. As meat cooks, the heat pulls open its pores, and the flavors of the rub seep right in.

Rubs help produce *bark,* a crisp and flavorful crust that also helps hold in meat's moisture.

You find out more about rubs in Chapter 5; Chapter 6 gives you recipes for rubs of all kinds.

Marinating: The power and the glory

Marinade, a light liquid that you soak meat in before you cook it, does as much good for the texture of meat as it does for the flavor.

Most marinades are made up of an acid (vinegar, lemon juice, or some such) and an oil. The acid helps break down the fibers to tenderize the meat, and oil helps hold the acid against the meat so it can do the most good. The rest is flavor — whatever combination of seasonings you like.

Marinades tend to work fast, propelling a lot of flavor and good tenderizing effect into meat. They can be vehicles for intense tastes or subtle ones.

I tell you more about marinades in Chapter 5. In Chapter 7, you find recipes for marinades both traditional and exotic.

The big finish: Sauces

You can call pretty much anything liquid a *sauce,* and depending on who or where you are, your definition of true barbecue sauce may be very different. (Get a taste of those differences in "Touring the Four All-American Barbecue Regions," earlier in this chapter.)

Different kinds of sauces are appropriate at different stages of the cooking process. You don't put a sugary sauce on food before it has been cooked through, for example, because it burns right around it.

In Chapter 8, I fill you in on the ways you create and use various kinds of sauces. Then in Chapters 9 through 11, I give you a slew of recipes for sauces of all kinds from each of the barbecue regions and beyond.

How the Big Guns of Barbecue Do What They Do

Prying pointers out of barbecue cooks is no easy task. Secretiveness is part of the fun and show of barbecue. Cooks guard their sauce recipes and rub mixtures with the ferocity of a mother bear guarding her cubs, but they throw in taunts and flat-out lies to toy with their predators.

Are the recipes in this book exactly as their authors make them? Hardly. You can bank on their being amended just enough so that you get a great result that's not *quite* the one the recipe's author gets. (All the more reason to play around and make it your own, as I recommend in the upcoming section, "Getting Creative As You Cook.")

Tomato or not tomato — that is the question

Barbecue may well have been around since the 17th century, and although tomatoey barbecue sauce has for much of the eating (if not barbecue-cooking) public become synonymous with *barbecue,* tomatoes were a much later introduction to the cooking style.

Although plenty of evidence shows that they were eaten elsewhere earlier, tomatoes didn't become a staple in American kitchens until the mid-19th century. That may be because of legends that they were poisonous. Depending on whom you ask, that myth took hold because the plant is a member of the nightshade family, which includes truly poisonous plants, or because the high acid content caused lead to leach out of flatware and cause sickness.

Another legend has it that Puritans turned up their noses at the tomato because it was thought to have aphrodisiacal properties. (In French, the tomatoes were referred to as pommes d'amour, or love apples.)

Tomatoes therefore came late to barbecue (but came with a vengeance, if the lineup of sauces on grocery store shelves is to be believed). The first settlers in the eastern region of the Carolinas wouldn't have even considered adding tomatoes to their sauces. To this day, the preference in the Carolinas is for vinegar- or mustard-based sauces.

Despite all the big talk and the energy spent hanging on to signature recipes, the truth of the matter is this: About 95 percent of what everybody does is the same. The nuances make for different flavors, slightly juicier meat, a nominally sweeter smoke flavor, and a ton of bullshitting over beers.

So, no, you don't get every detail you might want from a successful barbecue cook, but you get what you need. In the upcoming chapters, I share that information with you — details about choosing wood for smoking, as well as balancing a rub, marinade, or sauce, and more.

Concocting rubs and sauces

Even though sauce recipes are held precious, the basic formula for creating sauces gives you everything you need to know to start working out your own recipe (which you, in turn, can refuse to share).

Any sauce starts with a *base* that provides the underlying flavor and holds everything together. That base may be ketchup, vinegar, mustard, tomato paste, chili sauce, or anything along those lines (or a combination of all of them). From there, add some sweetness with sugar or molasses, and then throw in the spices you like. I give you a lot more detail about building sauces in Chapter 8, and you find sauce recipes of every stripe in the rest of Part III.

They may not admit it to you, but a lot of competitive barbecue cooks start out with bottled sauce and doctor it to their taste. Playing around with a sauce you know and enjoy is an easy way to start experimenting without investing too much time in building sauce from scratch.

Rubs follow more or less the same formula, starting with something fairly neutral that will mix easily with the primary flavors you want in the rub. Paprika generally fills this slot. To that, you add salt, sugar, and whatever combination of spices tickles your fancy. You want something with a little kick, like cayenne pepper, chili powder, or even curry powder, and you want some lower-profile seasonings like cumin, black pepper, or garlic powder. You can toy around with it easily until you like the way it hits your tongue.

Chapter 5 runs down the finer points of putting together a solid rub from scratch.

From meat to magic

The slow-cooking process that takes even the saddest cut of meat and turns it into a dream-invading delicacy relies on time and a steady temperature. The equipment you use to make that happen depends on how much and how often you intend to cook, along with how much money you want to spend.

The unfortunate fact is that the less-expensive versions actually require the most barbecue smarts to produce great results. Spend more money, and you usually get better temperature control. Without that, you end up a slave to your thermometer, regularly checking in and adjusting your vents or adding charcoal to bring the temperature back to its sweet spot.

Reasonably good barbecue smokers start out at around $200, and high-end equipment can easily cost tens of thousands of dollars. You find out about choosing a smoker in Chapter 2. Using one to its best advantages is a topic I cover in Chapter 4.

Getting Creative As You Cook

Color me slow, but I'd been out on my own for several years before I figured out that a recipe was just a suggestion, not a make-or-break set of dictates. Cooking became a lot more fun when I realized that tripling the garlic or cutting back on sugar were fine-and-dandy ideas that led to results that I preferred over the original recipes.

This book has a ton of recipes, but cooking that's limited to a list of directions has little pleasure in it. I hope you use this book as a jumping-off point to creating the rub, sauce, or marinade that strikes you just right.

Behind every great recipe: An experiment

Chocolate chips came about because Ruth Graves Wakefield tried a last-minute substitution. Thinking semisweet chocolate would melt into her cookie batter, she was surprised to pull from her oven blonde cookies with chocolate bits sprinkled throughout them. That was in the 1930s. Today, chocolate chip cookies are the world's most popular.

No doubt some experiments yield results you couldn't, in good conscience, feed to friends. Even if only one out of five tries gave you something to brag about, going out on a limb would pay off. But by using the advice in this book, which includes basic tenets to blend rubs and marinades by (Chapter 5) and standards by which to stir up sauces (Chapter 8), you have all the information you need to proceed down the do-it-yourself route without worry.

When you have a little information about how and why the components of barbecue do what they do, you can confidently put your own signature on any of them. Barbecue is all about bragging rights. You can't earn them without a little experimentation.

Benefiting from others' trial and error

Turns out mint doesn't belong in a spice rub. It gets bitter and doesn't play well with other common seasonings. Now you know, and you don't have to make that mistake.

Given that barbecue has been a mainstay of American cuisine for centuries, a lot of knowledge has built up around it (despite cooks' best efforts to guard their secrets). Rely on the tidbits that you find throughout the book to guide your own forays into cooking.

Others' missteps mean you're every bit as free to experiment but can do so with less fear of retribution from the tasters. This book gives you advice and recipes you can rely on to make cooking as fun as eating.

Incorporating contemporary and exotic recipes

Many of the techniques that are now intrinsic to barbeque started out in other areas of the world or drew upon cooking knowledge passed through centuries and from family to family or culture to culture. But cooking techniques and trends change all the time — especially given the current boom of food TV and the endless food-centered Web sites and blogs.

If you're cooking to satisfy a barbecue competition judge, you'll follow a strict set of rules outlining what barbecue really is and is not, but if you're cooking just to satisfy yourself and your friends, then the only rules that matter are yours.

The recipes in this book pull some long-lost influences back into the barbecue fold and throw in some modern twists, too, by calling on a couple great chefs who know at least as much about how barbecue happens in Korea as they do about Carolina or Memphis methods.

Experimentation is a big part of the spirit of barbecue, and I hope you find in this book the inspiration and means for running some experiments of your own.

Chapter 2

Gathering Must-Have Equipment

- -

In This Chapter

▶ Choosing your weapon: Smokers and grills

▶ Getting the lowdown on charcoal

▶ Barking up the right tree: Wood for smoking

▶ Having on hand the right tools for each stage of the game

- -

*U*nless you're strictly a microwave "cook," you probably already have much of the equipment you need to get started with the recipes in this book. Barbecue isn't so esoteric that you have to run out and buy a bunch of special tools to give it a go.

If you end up taking to barbecue (and be warned, it becomes an obsession or even a lifestyle for a pretty high percentage of harmless dabblers), you have no end of options for upgrading and expanding your tool kit, and more show up on the market almost daily.

In the meantime, start small. This chapter gives you what you need to know about the tools that are essential for barbecue cooking, and it fills you in on some of the options for the bigger, better, badder equipment that you may want to check into down the line.

Although a superfancy, high-end smoker looks awfully sexy and comes with features that you may find useful, some of the world's best barbecue comes off a homemade barrel smoker — the very antithesis of high-tech equipment. If you understand the concepts behind barbecue, you can make it happen in the most dire of equipment circumstances.

Settling on a Smoker

Back in ye olden days, people dug a pit to smoke meats, so don't think you have to drop a heap of dollars on your equipment. Using less-expensive options may mean that you have to work a little harder and be a little more watchful to keep the temperature steady. What it doesn't mean is that you can't cook great barbecue, so don't be a sissy. As I show you, even a charcoal grill can serve as a smoker.

The following sections give you some ideas about what you can do with the various kinds of equipment available and what makes them desirable or not.

Rigging a charcoal grill

Using a charcoal grill as a smoker is a good way to test the barbecue waters. If you find you enjoy smoking, you're likely to want to upgrade, but a large kettle grill with a lid is a reasonable starting point.

The main difference between grilling and barbecue is that when you grill, you cook directly over the heat source. Barbecue cooking uses indirect heat. To make that happen in a grill, do the following:

1. **Prepare your heat source.**

   Use a chimney starter (see "Using a chimney starter," later in this chapter) to light your charcoal.

2. **Place the charcoal.**

   When it's ready, heap the hot charcoal onto only one side of the kettle's bottom grate, leaving the other side free for the meat.

3. **Add wood.**

   Put soaked wood chunks or an aluminum-foil packet of wood chips directly onto the coals, as Figure 2-1 shows you. (Check out "Using wood to add flavor," later in this chapter, for more details)

4. **Get ready to cook.**

   Place the top grate onto the kettle and give it a few minutes to heat up.

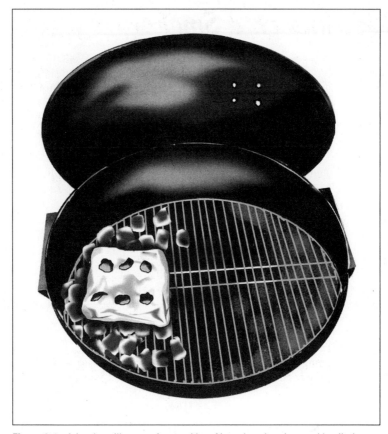

Figure 2-1: A kettle grill set up for smoking. Note that the charcoal is piled onto one side instead of across the bottom grate, as it would be for grilling.

5. **Throw your meat on the grate, carefully.**

   Place your meat on the side of the grill *opposite* the charcoal. Figure 2-2 shows you how your setup should look.

6. **Close the lid to smoke the meat.**

   Leave the vents or intake partially open to keep oxygen moving over the charcoal and to encourage good circulation of the heat throughout the grill. Adjust the upper vent or exhaust above the meat and opposite the fire to draw heat and smoke toward the meat.

Figure 2-2: Keep your meat out of the direct line of the heat source when you use your charcoal grill as a smoker.

Check the temperature intermittently by inserting a candy thermometer into the vent on the grill's lid. (Make sure the vent is positioned over the food that you're cooking so you know you're reading the temperature where you're most concerned about it.) Open the vents farther to increase heat, and narrow them to decrease it. Add more charcoal if you need to increase the heat by several degrees.

Because the heat is on only one side of the grill, you need to move your meat regularly so that each piece gets roughly the same amount of time next to the charcoal. Doing so helps you cook your food evenly.

Buying a charcoal smoker

You most often run into two varieties of charcoal smokers for home cooks on the commercial market:

- ✔ **Vertical smoker:** A vertical smoker (sometimes called a *bullet smoker* because of its shape; see Figure 2-3) is one of the all-time most popular smokers and not terribly hefty in size or cost. You use it by cooking a significant distance over the heat and with a water pan in between the heat source and the cooking grate to keep the meat moist.

- ✔ **Offset horizontal smoker:** An offset horizontal smoker (see Figure 2-3) keeps the fire in a compartment separate from the meat. You have a large cooking surface and vents to control the heat and keep it moving through the cooking chamber.

Figure 2-3: On a vertical smoker (left), the meat cooks far above the heat. An offset horizontal smoker separates the fire and the cooking surface.

Building a barrel smoker

A do-it-yourself option if you're industrious, a *barrel smoker* makes use of a 55-gallon drum turned on its side and split down the middle (see Figure 2-4). This type of smoker is the definition of inexpensive, but it's fickle to use and doesn't last terribly long. It does have a heckuva cowboy quality, if that's what you're into. A number of Web resources are available to show you how to turn a barrel into a smoker; you can find a particularly thorough version for building a double-barrel smoker at `www.mikesell.net/smoker`.

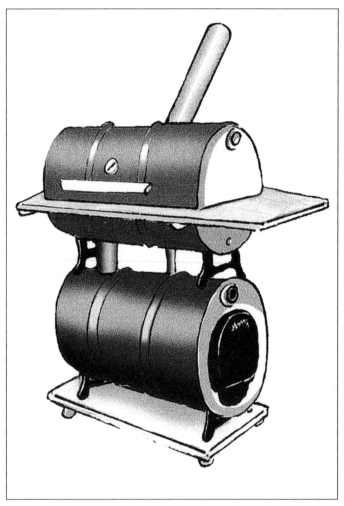

Figure 2-4: A barrel smoker is the rustic version of commercial horizontal smokers.

Using an electric or gas smoker

Take charcoal out of the equation, and you lose a lot of the great smoke flavor that makes barbecue an obsession for eaters and cooks. You can use wood with an electric or gas smoker (see Figure 2-5), but the effect is just not the same. (Although some barbecue cooks argue this point, as they do nearly every other point, most prefer to cook with charcoal to enhance the flavor of the smoke.)

Figure 2-5: You find gas and electric smokers in a range of styles.

What you gain from electric or gas smokers is easier-to-control heat. Instead of messing with adding charcoal, you just adjust a dial. Shazam!

Fire, Starters: Managing Heat

In most cases, you use charcoal as your heat source, and you use wood to add smoke and flavor. Why not use wood as heat and smoke, you ask? Because oversmoking is a common mistake when you try to kill two birds with one pile of wood — you have better luck and better smoke and heat control if you use charcoal. Use too much smoke, and you're likely to end up with a very unwelcome bitterness in your meat.

Eyeing charcoal types

You can buy charcoal in two varieties, both of which have their enthusiasts:

- ✔ **Charcoal briquettes:** Made from charred hardwood and coal, charcoal briquettes are the most commonly used medium for backyard grilling. Briquettes are in many cases eschewed by serious barbecue cooks because of the additives that are compressed into them to keep the briquettes burning and hold them together.

- ✔ **Lump charcoal:** Made from charred hardwood and nothing else, lump charcoal doesn't have the additives you find in charcoal briquettes (nor does it have the smooth shape — hence, the name). Lump charcoal burns hotter and faster than briquettes. You pay more for it, but depending on the sensitivity of the meat you're cooking, lump charcoal may be worth the expense for the lack of chemical additives that may flavor the meat.

If you choose to use charcoal briquettes (and plenty of great barbecue cooks do), make sure you avoid the kind with the lighter fluid built right in. The chemicals that help you light it burn right off the briquettes and waft into your food, giving it an acrid taste that only a masochist is going to find delightful. Using lighter fluid straight from the squeeze bottle is a bad idea as well and for the same reason. Check out the next section, "Using a chimney starter," to find out the best way to get charcoal burning without adding unwanted flavor.

Using a chimney starter

Through the magic of a chimney starter, you can light charcoal easily and quickly without pouring on the lousy-tasting chemicals you find in lighter fluid. You can buy a chimney starter (see Figure 2-6) at most hardware or home-supply stores.

You use it by stuffing newspaper into the bottom section and filling the top section with charcoal. Set it in a safe place and light the newspaper. In 15 to 20 minutes, your coals are ready to go. Just dump them into the smoker.

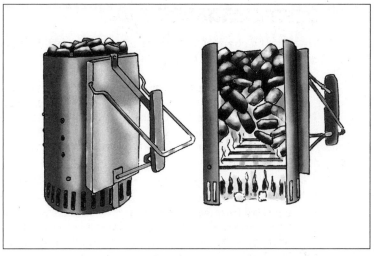

Figure 2-6: A chimney starter gets your coals ready for cooking without adding chemicals.

Determining how much charcoal you need

The amount of charcoal that you use varies according to whether you go for the lump or briquette variety and what and how much you're cooking. That's a lot of variables, and finding just the right amount of charcoal for reaching your target temperature takes some practice.

 Increasing heat is easier than reducing it, so proceed cautiously with charcoal. Start out with slightly less than you think you need and add more if it becomes necessary.

Wood: To Hickory or Not to Hickory

The meat of the matter, when it comes to barbecue, actually is the wood. Smoke gives barbecue its unique flavor, and you get the smoke from putting hardwood between your charcoal and your meat so that the slow-burning wood sends its heavenly smoke up into whatever you're cooking.

Charcoal quantity: What's right for a butt may be wrong for a chop

The amount of charcoal you use depends on the density and weight of the meat you're cooking, and the efficiency of the smoker you use. As an example, in Tom's Weber Smokey Mountain Cooker, a metal ring at the base of the smoker sits on a rack. He typically smokes two to three pork butts at a time, each with an average weight of 6 pounds, so that's 12 to 18 pounds of pork. For that amount of meat, he fills the ring to the top, fills a chimney starter (check out the section "A Mop, Some Tongs, and So On," later in this chapter), lights that charcoal, and when it's hot, dumps it on top of the ring of briquettes.

"All said. I use about 65 percent of an 18-pound bag of briquettes," Tom explains. "It gets me about 12 hours of smoking, holding the temp to about 95 percent of the original set-point temperature. The smokers I use are extremely efficient with a fuel source. In fact I can put five butts (30 pounds) on that smoker with the same amount of coals."

Things change considerably if the smoker isn't as efficient. Tom remembers smoking about 70 pounds of meat on a custom rig: "It took me *three bags* — 54 pounds — of coals to smoke that for 12 hours," he said. "Very inefficient. If I smoked 70 pounds of meat across two units like mine, I could do it with about 30 total pounds of coals. My competition units ($225 apiece) are much more efficient than the custom, and larger capacity rig, I used ($6,000!)."

Meat density is another variable to consider. A pork butt is the size of a football and very dense. Say it weighs about 6 pounds, meaning you need about 12 hours to smoke it. Three slabs of ribs with bones weigh 6 pounds, too, but they need only 4 to 6 hours to smoke. Cook 18 ½-pound pork chops, and that particular 6 pounds' worth of meat needs only 3 to 4 hours on the smoker.

The single butt takes 8 pounds of briquettes; the pork chops and ribs need only about 3 to 4 pounds of briquettes. Tom's rough rule of thumb: About a dozen briquettes for a pound of meat *minus the bone weight* to slow-cook meat.

Using wood to add flavor

You can add wood to your grill or smoker in a couple different forms:

- ✔ **Chips** are small pieces along the lines of mulch. Wrap them in heavy-duty aluminum foil and tear several holes in the foil to give the smoke a route out of the packet and onto your meat. A word of warning: Fish easily picks up a metallic flavor from the foil, so if you're planning to smoke fish, you may want to use wood chunks instead.

- ✔ **Chunks** are good-sized pieces of wood that are 3 or 4 inches across. Before you use them, soak them in cold water for half an hour to an hour. Drain off the excess water and then place the chunks right on top of your charcoal.

 Avoid using softwood to smoke meat. Pine trees and other conifers smell great, but they do terrible things to the taste of meat. Any seasoned hardwood is fair game. The next section, "Describing characteristics of woods," gives you a rough idea of what different woods will do for your barbecue.

Describing characteristics of woods

You carefully choose your marinade, your meat, your rub — and the decisions don't stop there. The type of wood you use to smoke meat affects the way it tastes.

Here's a rundown of the characteristics you find in different types of wood:

- ✔ **Almond** or **pecan** wood imparts a mild, nutty (surprise!) taste.
- ✔ **Apple** and **cherry** woods do what their fruits would: They give a sweet, fruity flavor.
- ✔ **Hickory** provides an intense flavor; be careful not to use too much.
- ✔ **Maple** is mild and versatile, and its smoke is a little sweet.
- ✔ **Oak** is a finicky option because it has a distinct flavor that can easily come across too strong.
- ✔ **Walnut** comes off as bitter if you use too much of it. Better to use it restrainedly and with a milder choice, like one of the fruit woods.

A Mop, Some Tongs, and So On

Ours is an age of excess. Along with completely unnecessary tools for golfers, wine drinkers, and virtually every other hobbyist from hunters to knitters, barbecue cooks have a steady stream of new and "life-altering" gadgets to choose from. Some of these options may tempt you mightily, but very few of them do you actually need.

In this section, I run down the equipment you'll use over and over in your barbecue cooking.

Make sure you get your hands on the following before you begin cooking:

- **Smoker or grill:** You get a rundown of your smoker options in the "Settling on a Smoker" section, earlier in this chapter. There, I also tell you how to use your grill to approximate the effect of a smoker so you can try it out before committing to the cost of buying your own.

- **Fire:** You need matches or a long butane lighter to get your charcoal going.

- **Charcoal:** I tell you everything you need to know about your heat source in the "Fire, Starters: Managing Heat" section, earlier in this chapter.

- **Chimney starter:** A chimney starter is the best way to get your charcoal going. (Check out the "Using a chimney starter" section, earlier in this chapter, to get the details on chimney starters.")

- **Tongs and a long-handled metal spatula:** Only suckers turn meat with a fork. You don't want to pierce it and let the juices run out. Tongs or spatulas (see Figure 2-7) let you move meat without damaging it.

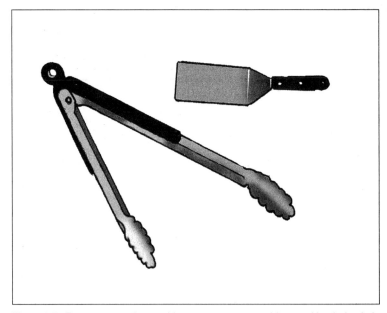

Figure 2-7: Tongs or spatulas enable you to turn meat without poking holes in it.

✔ **Basting brush or mop:** Choose a sturdy brush or buy a cotton basting mop (see Figure 2-8), which gives you great coverage quickly — a plus considering you're working hard to maintain a steady temperature.

✔ **Thermometer:** If your smoker doesn't have a built-in thermometer, stick a candy thermometer into a vent. You find digital, dial, and notched versions (see Figure 2-9). Take your pick; they all suit your purposes just fine.

✔ **Grill brush:** No matter how spectacular your last batch of ribs was, it's not going to taste good on today's chicken. A gunked-up grate makes meat stick and causes you extra headache because you have to keep the lid open longer and lose valuable heat while you wrestle the meat as you move it during cooking. A thorough scrape with a grill brush (see Figure 2-10) goes a long way toward maintaining the flavor of your food and keeping it from sticking.

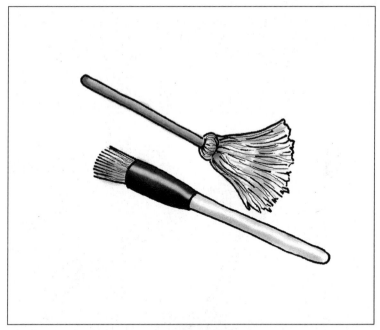

Figure 2-8: A well-made brush or basting mop allows you to quickly sauce whatever you're cooking.

Figure 2-9: Thermometers come in three flavors: digital, dial, and notched.

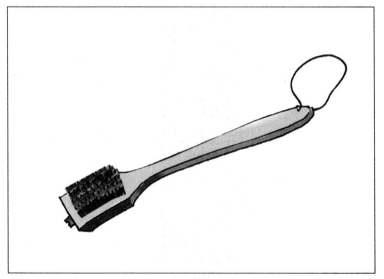

Figure 2-10: Get rid of residue with a grill brush.

Estimating temperature in a pinch

If ever you find yourself without a thermometer but otherwise ready to cook, no need to run out for a replacement — use the "hands-on" method to estimate the temperature of your heat source. Hold your hand approximately 5 to 6 inches above the coals; the amount of time you can stand to keep it there tells you your temperature range. If you can hold your hand above the coals for

✔ 1 to 2 seconds, the coals are hotter than 500 degrees

✔ 3 to 4 seconds, you're working with medium grill heat at about 350 to 400 degrees

✔ 6 seconds or so, and you've got smoking heat — 250 degrees or less

✔ **Drip pan:** Dripping fat and charcoal are not a good combination. Keep the two separate by using a drip pan. A pie tin or cake pan or a pan you fashion from heavy-duty aluminum foil works great.

✔ **Spray bottle:** Use a spray bottle to discourage flames that may lick up from your grill or to add moisture to meat as you smoke it.

✔ **Apron:** In addition to making you look sexy, aprons give you a place to stash your tongs and a way to save your clothes from all manner of stains.

✔ **Heat-resistant gloves:** Big cuts of meat need hands-on attention, which means you need heat-resistant gloves so you can move them.

✔ **Heavy-duty aluminum foil:** You use foil to wrap meat before you cook it and to keep the meat hot for residual cooking after it's out of the smoker or off the grill.

✔ **Plastic wrap:** You need it to cover marinating meat or for storing cooked food.

✔ **Glass bowls:** When you marinate meat, do it in a glass container. Stainless steel works, too, but steer clear of aluminum or cast iron, which react with the marinade and knock it out of whack.

✔ **Sharp knives:** You're going to need to trim your meat with some precision and in some cases around tricky terrain. A boning knife gets into hard-to-navigate spots, and an 8-inch chef's knife works well for outside trimming (see Figure 2-11).

You can use whatever knives you feel comfortable with — just make sure they're sharp. Dull knives not only make trimming a challenge, they also put you in danger of gouging yourself as you fight through the meat.

Figure 2-11: A chef's knife and a flexible boning knife are good choices for trimming fat from meat.

Chapter 3

Collecting Ingredients and Using Them Wisely

*B*arbecue comes very close to turning the sow's ear of metaphor into a silk purse. It takes otherwise unpleasant-to-eat cuts of meat and turns them delicious. Still, starting with the right ingredients makes the alchemy more certain.

If you're going to put forth the effort to cook, give your energies their due by using the best ingredients you can get your hands on. That doesn't necessarily mean spending a fortune, but it does mean choosing wisely. This chapter equips you to start your meals right with a foundation of great ingredients.

You put a lot of time and energy into your cooking, so give your efforts their due by using ingredients that support rather than supplant them.

Finding Meat That Makes the Cut

How you plan to cook has a lot to do with the cut of meat you want to buy. Anything cut from the midsection of an animal's back — tenderloin, sirloin, and ribs, for example — works best when it's cooked quickly, over high heat. (For grilling or searing, common knowledge says that you stay as far as possible from the hoof and the horns. That pretty much leaves the middle of the back.)

Cuts of meat that come from the part of the animal that did most of the work (the shoulders and legs) are just right for barbecue cooking, which breaks down the tough muscle by keeping it over low heat for a good long time.

The front of an animal is the part that does the work and, therefore, has the strongest muscle. More muscle means more collagen, and more collagen means less tenderness. Enter barbecue: Cooking muscle-heavy cuts of meat for a long time over low heat breaks down the collagen.

More fat means more flavor

Fat means energy for a living animal, which builds stores of the stuff. And for an animal that later takes a turn as food, that same fat means flavor and moisture. Without it, meat tends toward the tough, bland, and dry.

Muscle fibers have much the same consistency from animal to animal. Muscles do what they do in the same manner, whether that project is powering a wing or driving a lope across the meadow. Fat cells are where the differences among meat come into play. Because they're the closets of biochemistry, storing any fat-soluble matter the animal takes in, they reflect the animal's eating habits and the intestinal *microbes* (microscopic organisms that contribute to digestion, as well as the fungi and viruses that cause illness) that make it into its digestive tract.

Because fat stores hang onto food energy, they also maintain any flavor from that food that's fat soluble. You see "grass-fed" advertised so often on beef packaging because that diet is not just more natural for the cattle but tends to produce a more flavorful beef.

Big sheets of fat serve a purpose on cuts like brisket, which has a blanket of fat that covers the cut. (Check out the upcoming "Brisket" section.) That fat layer melts as the brisket heats up and drips down into the meat to keep it flavorful and moist.

What you want in every cut of pork, lamb, or beef is good *marbling* — the network of meandering veins of thin fat that run throughout the cut. This kind of fat feeds the meat moisture and flavor, giving it a toothsome texture.

As animals age, they build stores of fat in their muscles as energy reserves. These stores show up as thick deposits in the meat, and they aren't as beneficial as the thinner, more evenly distributed marbling that you want to look for. The veins of fat break up the strong, chewy muscle tissue and add juiciness as they melt during cooking.

Fresher is better

After meat is portioned and packaged, it's delicate as a diva, easily falling prey to bacteria, unsavory flavors in your fridge, and oxidation.

Refrigeration slows down meat's inevitable decay, and freezing temporarily stops it. But freezing is hard on meat. Low temperatures irretrievably change meat's composition, and the difference shows up as less-tender meat: Ice crystals grow from the meat's juices and drill holes that later leak the precious fluids that keep meat from becoming tough as it cooks.

And then there's *freezer burn,* the discoloration that arises from extreme loss of moisture after meat has spent too much time in the freezer. Freezer-burnt meat inevitably has a tough texture and suspect flavor.

No matter what meat you're buying, don't forget to eyeball the sell-by date on the label to make sure that day hasn't come and gone.

Making friends with your butcher certainly doesn't hurt. Customers of local butcher shops generally find services and perks they'd never have expected from large chain meat counters.

Running Down the Options, Cut by Cut

The beauty of barbecue is that it's infinitely adaptable, so this section by no means gives you the full spectrum of meat cuts, but it does give you an introduction to the most-cooked cuts for traditional barbecue cooking.

Pork

Look for pork that has a faint pink color. Darker meat means older meat: Either it came from an older pig that had more time to develop tough muscle, or it was cut and exposed to air for a longer time than is ideal. Too much juice surrounding the meat is never a good thing, nor is juice that's cloudy.

Shoulder

The shoulder area yields two cuts, Boston butt (so-named not for the hog's hindquarters but for barrels the cut was stored and shipped in back in ye olden times) and the picnic shoulder. Both commonly are used for pulled pork, and they're good for non-barbecue applications like stewing.

Boston butt is the more tender of the two cuts. Picnic shoulder cuts cost lest but contain more large fat deposits. Figure 3-1 gives you a look at both cuts.

Ribs

Pork ribs are cut from either the top or bottom portion of the rib cage. Baby back, or loin back, ribs come from the top section and are small and pretty lean, which makes them faster to cook. Spareribs come from the area closer to the belly, which makes them a neighbor to the bacon area and, as you may expect, fattier than baby back ribs. You see an example of both rib cuts in Figure 3-2.

Beef

You want any beef that you buy to have a rosy hue and abundant marbling (see Figure 3-3). The exception is vacuum-packed beef, which retains the purplish color that beef has before it's exposed to air. Pass over any beef that has a gray or brown tinge to it.

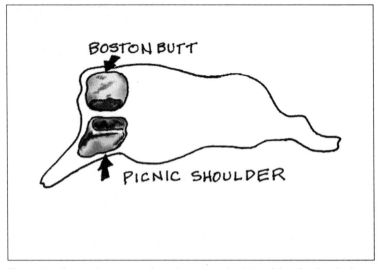

Figure 3-1: Boston butt comes from the upper shoulder of the pig; the picnic shoulder comes from the joint area of the foreleg.

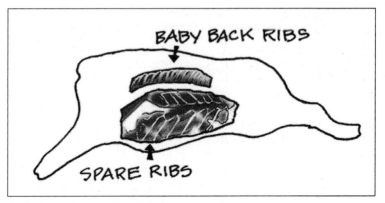

Figure 3-2: The ribs yield two different cuts. Leaner baby back ribs come from the top and spareribs from the bottom.

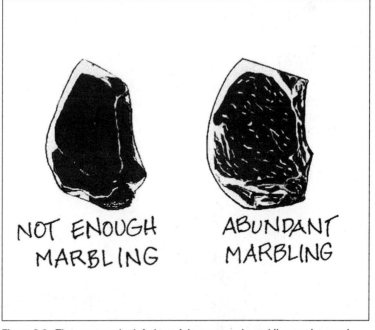

Figure 3-3: The meat on the left doesn't have enough marbling to give good flavor and texture; the cut on the right is perfect.

Meat should feel firm, and you want to buy cuts that aren't swimming in juices. Too much moisture often indicates that the meat got warmer than it should have.

You can figure out whether meat has been previously frozen by pressing your thumb onto its surface. If water pools into the indentation, the meat has taken a turn in the freezer.

Ribs

Back ribs come from the same spot that yields rib roasts or rib-eye steaks and have a goodly amount of fat. Basically scrap, the slabs tend not to have a lot of meat on them. Look for the meatiest cuts you can find. Ideally, you don't see the bones of the ribs on the slab.

Beef short ribs are cut into individual ribs (English style) or as cross-sections of rib meat with slices of bone dotting the cut (flanken style). You're more likely to use a rack of back ribs for barbecue cooking; the other cuts are ideal for *braising* (cooking slowly in a small amount of liquid).

Figure 3-4 shows you all three styles of beef ribs.

Brisket

Brisket is cut from about the same area of the cow that picnic shoulder comes from on a hog (see Figure 3-5). It's made up of a flat and a point (see Chapter 4). The point is thicker and holds a lot more fat than the flat, which is heftier. A fat cap runs along the top length of the brisket and is critical for keeping this otherwise tough cut of meat moist while it cooks.

Look for brisket with even marbling, a nice, white fat cap and uniform thickness throughout.

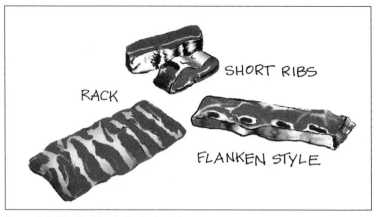

Figure 3-4: You find beef ribs in three forms.

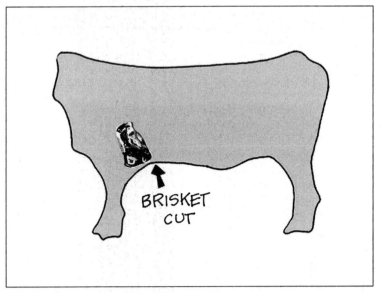

Figure 3-5: Brisket comes from atop the foreleg of the cow.

Poultry

In most cases, you leave a chicken or turkey whole when you cook it in the smoker. Butterflying the bird helps it cook faster and more evenly. (For information on how to butterfly a chicken or turkey, turn to Chapter 4.)

Chicken

 Look for a fryer chicken that weighs in somewhere close to 3 ½ pounds. The skin should be cream or slightly yellow in color, and any juices that surround the chicken are likely to be pink and clear. (Avoid chicken that has dark, foggy-looking juice or an excess of juice.)

Turkey

Turkeys need some kind of *brining* (soaking in salt and liquid) to stay juicy and flavorful. If you want to brine the bird yourself, go for a natural turkey; if you prefer to go straight to the rub portion of the program and then smoke the sucker, go ahead and buy a self-basted bird.

 Look for one weighing somewhere around 13 pounds. Buy one much bigger than that, and the bird is likely to dry out from the long cooking time you need to get the heat to its center.

Handling Meat without Hazard

So delicious, yet so very damaging to your intestines if not handled properly: Meat and its juices are perfect settings for bacteria that can put the hurt on you.

Raw meat is to bacteria like Barry White records and satin sheets are to humans. Food doesn't start out sterile (but high temperatures kill off most of the bacteria that rode along on your food from the farm to your kitchen), and protein in particular is a primo locale for encouraging bacteria to multiply.

None of this means you should shy away from meat, but it does mean that treating it with proper care is a must for the health of you and your guests.

Bacteria is most likely the culprit when the nastiness of foodborne illness (cramping, nausea, diarrhea, vomiting) invades your home. Handling food safely makes your chances of having to cope with these flulike symptoms much slimmer.

Follow these guidelines to ensure that you're not giving bacteria a playground while you prepare your meal:

✔ **Before you get started, wash in hot water all the utensils and surfaces you intend to use.** Bacteria may be hanging out on your cutting board before you even start.

✔ **Avoid cross-contamination:** Don't let anything touch the raw meat or its juices — or anything the meat and juices came into contact with.

- Use one knife and cutting board to cut vegetables and any other non-meat food, and use a separate knife and cutting board to prep your meat.

- Regard anything that the meat touches as out of commission for the rest of your prep work. If you set raw meat on a dish, that dish is exactly the wrong thing for ferrying your cooked food back from the grill.

- Wear gloves when you work with meat, or wash your hands thoroughly in hot water before you touch anything else.

- Portion out the amount of rub you think you need before you start. Throw out any leftovers from that portion. You can keep your rub, but not if it has come into contact with meat, and chances are good that the process of applying it leads to contamination from your hands.

✔ **Store meat at an appropriate temperature.** Refrigeration slows down bacteria, so keep meat at 40 degrees or lower until shortly before you want to cook it. (In Chapter 4, I tell you about the benefits of letting meat sit at room temperature before cooking. That's fine as long as you don't go overboard.) Throw out any meat that has been outside the fridge or freezer for more than two hours.

✔ **Throw out any leftover marinade.** It may have been your best batch ever, but if it came into contact with meat, it's fit only for the garbage disposal.

Stocking Dry Ingredients

In contrast to the bland look of herbs and spices as you so often see them — in rows of identical jars in grocery stores — herbs and spices have a long and colorful history of intrigue, one with power struggles, transcendence, and poetry. Seasonings have inspired dangerous travels, treated illnesses, fueled spiritual practices, and defined and refined cultures. More to the point here, they've transformed many a dinner from bland to enchanting.

The difference between herb and spice depends on where on a plant the flavorful bit originates:

✔ *Herbs* are the leafy green bits of plants that grow upright and aren't woody.

✔ *Spices* include plants' bark, seeds, roots, fruit, or flowers. Cinnamon comes from bark, for example; cloves are dried flower buds.

Must-haves for your spice cabinet

As you continue to cook, your stock of seasonings will grow. To get going, you want a collection of adaptable flavors in your spice rack. Here's a list of the seasonings you can't cook well without, the ones that provide the basis for your barbecue cooking collection:

✔ Allspice

✔ Black pepper

✔ Cayenne pepper

✔ Chili powder

✔ Cinnamon

✔ Cloves

✔ Coriander

✔ Crushed red pepper

✔ Cumin

✔ Curry powder

✔ Dry mustard

✔ Garlic powder

✔ Ginger

✔ Salt

✔ Sweet paprika

✔ Sugar

Spices can be extremely spendy, particularly if you buy them a little at a time. If you're even moderately committed to cooking, buy spices in bulk at discount stores. You end up paying about a tenth of what you would by using those teeny jars that the super-markets sell.

Storing spices, but not too long

Dried herbs and spices are pretty stable. You don't need to baby them, but a few tips go a long way toward keeping your seasonings at their flavorful best:

✔ **Avoid heat.** Ideally, you want your spices to stay under 70 degrees, so storing them next to your stove or oven is not the best way to go.

✔ **Keep dried herbs dry.** Moisture leads to mold; avoid it by storing your spices in airtight containers. If you keep your seasonings in the fridge or freezer (which frankly isn't the best idea, given the humidity of those environments), make sure you put them back right after you use them so condensa-tion doesn't get a chance to infiltrate your herb.

✔ **Let there be no light.** Light is hot, and it saps strength from your spices. Keep your herbs in a cupboard, safely tucked away from any light source.

✔ **Date your containers.** A safe bet is to throw away any spice that has reached its first birthday in your cupboard. When you buy a new container of this or that, mark the date on the label and save yourself any confusion or unsatisfying concoc-tions down the road.

If you can't smell it, you can't taste it. Whenever you're on the fence about throwing away a spice, take a whiff. Unless you get a clear waft of the aroma (and it's the one you want it to be), you can't expect to get the taste you're after from the seasoning. Toss it out.

The Stuff of Sauce

Given the importance of sauce in many barbecue enthusiasts' eyes, making your own may sound a little intimidating. Nuts to that.

Every great sauce follows a straightforward formula, and the differences among them come from the nuances — from basically the same stuff you'd do to tweak prepared barbecue sauce you picked up at the store.

In this section, I give you the basic ingredients for smart sauce-making. Balance is the critical element of sauce, and you find it by mixing sour, sweet, heat, and seasonings. In Chapter 11, you find guidelines for mixing and matching these components for killer sauces.

Even the most assiduous note-taking and recipe-following is unlikely to produce the same results in a sauce over and over. Sauces are greater than the sum of their parts and frankly feisty — their parts are in a battle; meanwhile you're working for balance. Getting a grip on how various flavors work together helps keep your sauces in line, and practice and experimentation make correcting to find the balance you want second nature.

Smart bases

The first rule of the sauce-making is to match your sauce to the stage of cooking during which you plan to use it: Add tomato-based barbecue sauce too early in the cooking process, for example, and you'll burn it onto your meat. (Chapter 1 tells you about how to use sauces at various stages.)

Every sauce starts with a base — a foundation ingredient that makes up the largest part of your recipe and carries the rest of the flavors.

How you like your sauce has a great deal to do with where you grew up. For many people, tomato-based sauce is the be-all and end-all of barbecue, but Carolinians would tell you differently. For them, sauce is thin and sour.

The skinny on fresh herbs

Dried herbs fill the bill for most of your barbecue projects, but you may at some point want to experiment with the fresh version. Especially if you have a garden — fresh herbs are much pricier than their dried and jarred counterparts.

The flavor in fresh herbs is not as concentrated, so you use more of fresh herbs than you do dried. If you're substituting fresh herbs in a recipe that calls for the dried version, a ratio of 1 teaspoon dried to 1 tablespoon fresh is about right in most cases.

Fresh herbs have a much shorter shelf life than do the dried varieties — about a week in the fridge. So if you find yourself swimming in fresh herbs and want to hang onto them, try drying them yourself. Here's how:

1. **Cut only healthy stems from the plant. Pick off any browned leaves from the stems.**

2. **Shake them to get rid of any dirt and bugs that may be clinging to the leaves. You also can rinse them in cold water, but be sure to blot off all the water with a paper towel.**

3. **Bundle several stems together, and tie the bundles with string near the cut end of the stems.**

4. **Hang the bundles in a dark spot that provides plenty of air circulation and little moisture.**

5. **Check back in five or six days. Complete drying may take a couple weeks. When the leaves are crumbly, you know the herbs are ready. Crunch 'em up and put 'em in an airtight container.**

Bases for barbecue sauces typically are one of the following, in order of most to least commonly used:

- ✔ **Tomato:** Sauce, paste, or ketchup — tomatoes provide a rich base that lends itself to sweet or hot sauces, and anything in between. Tomatoes are the most-used base for barbecue sauces.

- ✔ **Vinegar:** Thin, vinegar-based sauces have a (not surprisingly) strong, sour finish. Apple cider vinegar is the type most often called for. You can use these acidic sauces at any stage of the cooking process or as dips alongside your meat.

- ✔ **Mustard:** A great complement to pork, mustard-based sauces are thick and also can be used as marinade, mop, finishing sauce, or dip.

- ✔ **Mayonnaise:** Mayo-based "white sauce" is a favorite in the Alabama. Treat it like a tomato-based sauce and save it for the last few minutes of cooking.

Finding balance

When working toward balance in your sauce, you need sweet, savory, and sour elements, and you probably want a little something to give you heat.

Within those broad guidelines are about a gazillion possibilities, but keeping in mind those three elements when you're cooking can save your sauce from unpleasant imbalance. If something doesn't seem quite right, run through the elements and try to figure out which one's not pulling its weight.

No way can I give you a comprehensive list of bits that may improve your sauce, but in order to give you a notion of what kinds of things fit into each category, here are several ingredients that have been proven to do good things to a barbecue sauce:

✔ Sweet touches:

- Brown sugar

- Fruit juice

- Honey

- Molasses

- Soda (the Coke or Pepsi kind, not the fizzy water variety and not diet, which turns bitter when it cooks)

- Sugar

✔ Something sour:

- Lemon juice

- Lime juice

- Mustard

- Vinegar

- Worcestershire sauce

✔ Savory additions:

- Beef stock

- Chicken stock

- Ketchup

- Soy sauce

- Tomato paste

- Tomato sauce

Using seasonings

If it exists as a plant, someone at some time has thrown it into a sauce. Safe starts are anything that you'd use for a barbecue rub. Check out Chapter 5 for recommendations and to find out about flavor combinations that stand out — in good ways and in bad.

Season your sauces slowly. You can always add more, but taking some back is impossible.

Chapter 4

Barbecue Methods, Art, and Science

*B*efore you can offer your friends brisket so savory that they call upon the powers of interpretive dance to describe it, you have to gear up (see Chapter 2) and plan several steps ahead.

In this chapter, I give you guidelines for figuring out how to get where you want to go, from preparing the meat to taking that first taste. I also show you how to baby your barbecue while it cooks and how to finish it flavorfully without losing moisture.

Beginning with an End in Mind

If you're more inclined to jump in the car and start driving instead of planning a vacation, the type who might head down to the Little White Wedding Chapel with the person you just locked eyes with from across the paddy wagon, then barbecue may not be for you.

Barbecue requires forethought and patience — *good* barbecue, that is. You can make all the bad barbecue you want without planning and while in a hurry. You can also cook a turkey in the microwave, but no one's going to want to eat it.

When you get the hang of cooking barbecue, much of what you find in this section will be second nature. Your own adventures in trial and error will pay off and yield the secrets that make your cooking unique. Until you cook with confidence, though, take advantage of the hard work others have done.

Dedicate a notebook to your barbecue hits and misses. The glories that come off your grill or out of your pit unfortunately stick in your mind more as the *mmm*s of your guests than as the details of your efforts.

Planning hours (and hours) ahead

Despite the tales that need telling and the smack that needs talking, the real reason competitors show up for competitions a day before the cooking begins is that they need hours and hours to trim, marinate, smoke, and finish the meats they're sending to the judges.

The following sections give you some notion of how much time you need to set aside.

Seasoning with dry rubs

More time means more flavor, but some meats soak in rubs much more quickly than others and can become dry from the salt. To get the most out of your dry rubs without going overboard, stay within the following parameters:

- Allow about an hour and no more than an hour and a half for **chicken breasts.**

- Dark-meat chicken, such as **legs and thighs,** have muscle tissue that's less dense than that of the white meat, so they pick up flavors more easily. Forty-five minutes to an hour ought to do the trick.

- If you're cooking a **whole chicken,** 4 hours is a good start, and you can let the meat sit in its rub for as many as 12 hours.

- **Pork chops or steaks** need an hour and can handle as much as three hours.

- A **rack of ribs** does best with 12 hours.

- **Briskets and pork shoulders** require 12 hours and can handle a full day of soaking in a rub.

Use rubber gloves to pat rubs onto the meat you're cooking, and get rid of the gloves before you do anything else. Raw meat juices on your hands are the perfect route to contaminating your utensils or any other food you're cooking, adding up to a side of botulism with your brisket.

Using marinades

You find a wide range of possibilities with marinades, depending on the type and size of meat you're preparing and the ingredients in your marinade. Use a marinade with hot chilies and the meat needs to stay in contact with the marinade for a shorter time than it would if the strongest flavor in your marinade is oregano.

Another important factor is the size of the meat you're marinating:

- ✔ **Small pieces of meat, like shrimp or boneless chicken breasts,** grab flavors in about an hour.

- ✔ Give **steaks and chops** at least three hours and as many as six hours.

- ✔ **Veggies** do well with a couple hours' marinating time.

- ✔ **Whole chickens, pork loins, rack of lamb, or other big pieces of meat** need at least 5 hours and as many as 14 hours in the marinade.

- ✔ If you're marinating something as big as a **pork shoulder or brisket,** allow about a day.

Marinating is an art that requires trial and error. Let your imagination run wild as you concoct your own marinades (Chapter 5 gives you some starting points, and you find several recipes in Chapter 7), but remember when you use them that strong flavors make their presence known in a meat far faster than mild flavors do.

Selecting style and substance

The '80s proved that too much sometimes is more than enough, thank you. You're likely to dig up that same nugget of wisdom if you throw rub, marinade, and finishing sauce on a poor, defenseless chicken breast.

Chicken, fresh fish, and seafood put up little resistance to the flavors you add before you cook them. That's great news if you want to make something delicious in short order but bad news if you get overzealous with seasonings and marinating times.

How you choose to season your meats is one more in a long line of personal preference points that you encounter in the world of barbecue. You may well cook a rack of ribs that you marinate and rub and baste and then serve with a healthy mop of sauce. Then again, you may prefer your ribs to be simply rubbed and smoked.

Whatever methods you're using to get great flavor, you're thwarting yourself if you don't take harmony into consideration. Your best cinnamon-tinged rub just isn't going to work with the horse-radish in Alabama white sauce (see Chapter 9), no matter how delightful each is on its own.

Here's what you can expect from the various flavor-enhancing methods:

- **Dry rubs** provide dashes of flavor when you simply sprinkle them on and get cooking; they change the texture and character of meat when you use them as marinades. Dry rubs ensure that you get a nice crust on your smoked meats.

- **Marinades** tenderize meats because they have acids, like lemon juice or vinegar. Lean meats do especially well in marinades, which break down the muscle fibers and then keep the meat moist.

- **Finishing sauces** contain sugar, which means if you apply them before your meats are just about cooked, you get a burnt crust. Save finishing sauces for the final step, when they help keep meat moist. (I tell you more about finishing sauces in the "Using final-stage sauces" section, later in this chapter.)

Trimming and Prepping Meat without, Er, Butchering It

Striking the balance between juicy flavor and tender chewing starts with how you trim the meat you cook. The following sections give you guidelines for getting the most popular cuts ready for your rub or marinade — or grill or smoker.

Any piece of meat can stand a quick rinse in the sink to wash off odors or who-knows-what that the meat may have picked up in your fridge or the butcher's. Gently pat it dry after its light shower.

Priming pork butt

Pork butt actually comes from the shoulder of the animal and so contains a number of muscles that meet up in the cut (see Figure 4-1). It's a pretty solid hunk of meat, but one with a lot of fat veins that require a careful prep.

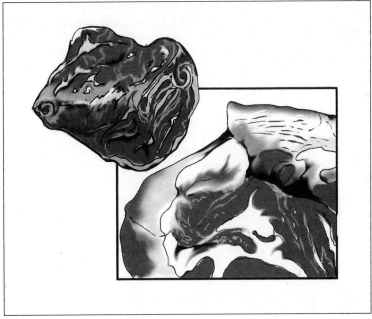

Figure 4-1: A pork butt comes with a thick fat cap and a lot of internal fat, as well.

When prepping a pork butt, take the following steps:

1. **Trim the fat cap.**

   Start at one side and, with a large, sharp knife, begin trimming the fat cap as evenly as possible about ⅛ inch all the way across the top.

2. **Cut off remaining pockets of fat.**

   You can make yourself crazy trying to scalpel through to get off all the fat you see on a pork butt, and there's just no good reason to do so. Slice off the substantial portions you find, and leave it at that.

3. **Cut out any large veins or blood clots you run into.**

Cleaning ribs

You don't have to work too hard to prep ribs, and you can use the process I outline here for beef or pork ribs.

Whatever style ribs you're making, you find a membrane along the bone side of the rack. Use a table knife (some people find a screwdriver works better) to puncture the membrane along one end of the rack, and then use a paper towel to grip the thing and pull it from the ribs (see Figure 4-2). Finally, if you see excess fat on the ribs, trim it off.

Preparing beef brisket

Brisket is cut from the sternum area of the cow, and it includes the following parts (see Figure 4-3):

- ✔ **Flat:** The lean meat that you slice and eat after you cook it

- ✔ **Point or deck:** A fattier section that overlays the majority of the flat

- ✔ **Fat cap:** The thick section of fat that separates the flat and the point

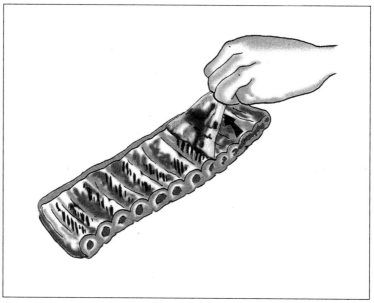

Figure 4-2: Pull the membrane from the bone side of the ribs before you season and cook them.

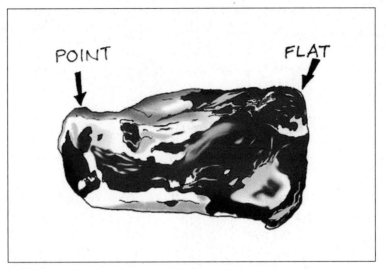

POINT   FLAT

Figure 4-3: Parts of a brisket.

Most brisket starts out with a fairly thick layer of fat. Start whittling that down by cutting off excess around the point. Then trim down the fat along the flat by running a large, sharp knife along the fat, leaving only about a quarter-inch layer. Rub your hand over the flat so you get a feel for any deep pockets of fat, and then shave those down.

Grooming poultry

A whole bird doesn't require much in the way of preparation. Just pull out the neck and giblets from the chicken's or turkey's cavity and then slice off whatever fat surrounds the opening. You don't need to tie up the legs as you would if you cooked it in the oven.

After you prepare a chicken, you may want to butterfly it to cook it more quickly and evenly. Here's how to do it:

1. **Set the chicken on the table so its back is facing up and its neck points away from you.**

2. **Use kitchen shears to cut alongside the backbone from end to end.**

   You cut through the ribs rather than the spine itself (see Figure 4-4).

Figure 4-4: Cut alongside a chicken's spine to split and flatten it for quicker cooking.

3. **Repeat Step 2, cutting along the opposite side of the spine to remove it completely.**

4. **Press down on the breastbone to flatten the chicken.**

Getting Time and Temperature Right

Some people tell you the secret to great barbecue is in the sauce. Great sauce helps, sure, but barbecue doesn't fly unless you cook it slowly, over low, indirect heat fueled by natural sources such as hardwood and charcoal.

Keeping a careful watch on the temperature in your smoker is critical for pulling tender, evenly cooked meat out of it. *When* you do the pulling is the difference between becoming Kansas City's pride and being told, "Next year, just bring the beer to the barbecue."

Determining cook time

Intuition and experience are enough for barbecue cooks with serious pit time under their belts, but target internal temperatures are the best guides for making your early barbecue efforts successful. Table 4-1 shows you the numbers you're shooting for.

The times that get you to the target internal temperature depend on the size and density of the meat that you're cooking and the cooking temperature (and its fluctuations).

Table 4-1	Target Temperatures
Meat	**Target Internal Temperature**
Beef brisket	185 to 195 degrees
Beef tenderloin	130 degrees for rare, 140 degrees for medium rare, 150 degrees for medium, 160 degrees for well
Boston butt	165 to 180 degrees if you're slicing it, 185 to 195 degrees for pulling
Pork shoulder	165 to 180 degrees if you're slicing it, 185 to 195 degrees for pulling
Whole chicken	170 degrees in the thigh
Whole hog	185 to 195 degrees in the shoulder
Whole turkey	170 degrees in the thigh

Managing the smoker

The urge to peek into or otherwise mess with your smoker is a strong one, but it's an impulse that's best beaten back. Use the Force, distract yourself with an unsolvable conundrum like whether free will exists if thought is dependent upon physical processes — whatever works — but for the love of Christmas, don't mess with the smoker any more than you have to.

For every single, solitary second your smoker lid is open, you lose 5 degrees of heat. You need several minutes to make up that loss.

Keeping an even temperature is your prime directive when it comes to slow smoking. Maintaining your target cooking temperature with as little volatility as possible is the most important thing you can do to end up with superstar-quality meat.

If you spend $10,000 on a barbecue pit, the thing should hold your temperature well. Along the spectrum of smoker types and qualities, you find varying degrees of temperature management. Unless you're already making money from your barbecue, I recommend sticking with something a few steps above the low end. You have to keep an eye on it, but you don't have to hock your grandfather's watch for it. (Chapter 2 tells you about choosing a smoker.)

Remember the following tips about holding a temperature in your smoker:

- Your target temperature for most meats is 225 degrees, and you have only about 25 degrees' leeway in either direction to stay in the comfort zone.

- If your smoker doesn't have a built-in thermometer, stick a candy thermometer through the vent to keep tabs on the inside temperature.

- Charcoal dies out after about 45 minutes, and you need a half-hour to get another batch ready. (You don't want to use charcoal that hasn't started to ash over.)

Free ribs, and no charge for the lies

Come summer, any old barbecue fan can take advantage of the free-for-all that arises at barbecue competitions. Because the competitors don't get vending licenses for the events, they can't sell their extra ribs, and they usually have quite a pile of them: Smoking a half-dozen racks is common, even though the judges evaluate only six ribs at most sanctioned events. Competitors want to improve their chances for getting that perfect pair of ribs.

In the moment of relief after their entries are turned in, many competitors hand out samples to passersby. Take advantage of the pulled pork or chicken, but take anything you hear from the source with a grain of salt.

Part of the fun of competing is blowing smoke and, even though you aren't a competitor at the moment, who's to say you won't be later? Tom Schneider, a contributor to this book and an accomplished pit master in the Indianapolis area warns first-timers not to be fooled by the friendly faces:

Barbecuers are some of the nicest, friendliest people around. They'll help you if you run out of ice or out of salt, but if you ever ask someone to give a piece of advice on barbecuing, you usually get a smile and not much more than that. If you do get more, chances are, that person is intentionally leading you down the path of screwing up your food.

✔ To keep a steady supply of ready charcoal, light another batch in a charcoal chimney (scc Chapter 2) shortly after you move a new batch into the smoker.

✔ Close down the upper dampers when you need to reduce the heat, and open them a bit when you want to raise the temperature.

✔ Seriously: Don't open the lid unless you absolutely have to. Otherwise, you're making your temperature (and, therefore, your meat) go wonky.

The Big Finish

Given the extensive amount of time you put into your barbecue, you wouldn't be the first person to melt into a puddle of glum if your food doesn't come out like you envisioned. Avoid that outcome by playing the barbecue endgame with good sense and patience.

You don't sprint to the barbecue finish. You keep on babying your meats until they're safely on your grateful guests' plates.

Using final-stage sauces

The sauce you coat your pulled pork in or slather on your ribs usually is not the sauce you use before or during cooking, and here's why: Any sauce that contains sugar or tomatoes is going to burn at a very low temperature, adding an unpleasant flavor and imparting a less-than-toothsome texture to your meats.

So what's the story with those sweet, tomato-based sauces that, for many people, are the essence of barbecue? Those are all well and good, provided that you wait until the cooking is almost done to use them.

 Baste your meat or brush on a mop sauce during cooking, but save the finishing sauce (meaning anything with sugar or tomatoes — most bottled sauces) for the last 10 percent of cooking time. Brushing it on at the end means it keeps the flavor you want instead of morphing into something that tastes like you should have used it to nourish your garden. Chapter 10 gives you recipes for mop sauces.

Keeping basting brushes clean

A challenge on par with creating the perfect sauce is cleaning the basting brush you use to apply it.

Oil clings to the bristles and doesn't rinse out no matter how determinedly you may attack the brush-cleaning process. Bristles stay sticky and may even stink up your utensil drawer.

Try putting your washed brushes in a glass, bristle-side-down, and pouring coarse salt in around them until salt covers the bristles. Just as it does with meat, salt pulls out moisture from the brushes so they're dry and ready to go when next you need them. Just shake off the salt.

Resting the meat

Just because you've pulled it from the smoker doesn't mean your meat is ready to go. Whatever you're cooking needs a moment to ease away from its cooking temperature and absorb the juices that otherwise would end up all over a plate instead of in the meat, where you want them. *Resting* your cooked meat — letting it sit away from the heat for a while — keeps it from drying out.

Proteins inside the meat change their shape in response to heat. Whatever moisture they hold is squeezed out in the process and ends up in the center of the meat, where temperatures are coolest. Give the meat a chance to cool down after cooking, and the proteins shift shape again, this time picking up moisture from the center of the meat.

Slice into meat before giving it a chance to rest, and you lose almost half the juices.

You invest way too much time in barbecue to let last-minute impatience ruin your work. Give your meats a good rest after cooking, and your efforts are better showcased. Count on about two minutes for each pound of meat that you cooked.

Some people tell you to tent your meat with aluminum foil while it rests. Others say that's just playing with it. The idea is that the foil keeps the heat in and keeps the meat from cooling off too fast. Maybe so, but the difference isn't striking. Foil or don't — this decision isn't going to make or break your results. But, of course, there's an exception. . . .

When you cook brisket or pork shoulder, you may want to wrap the meat tightly in foil and towels and let it sit in an insulated bag or cooler for an hour or so. Doing so takes advantage of *carryover cooking* (the high temperature that meat maintains even after it's away from the heat source), and it may help tenderize it. Depends on who you ask.

Pulling, slicing, presenting

After your meat is rested (I beg you: Check out the "Resting the meat" section if you don't know what I mean), you may well be finished. You
can simply toss ribs or chicken pieces on a plate. Other cuts require a smidge more work.

For pulled meats or brisket, find your knives or rubber gloves and take the following steps for getting your meat ready to serve:

- When pork shoulder for **pulled pork** is cool enough you can touch it, remove any fat still on the meat, and then dig in with your hands, removing bones and shredding the meat into thin strips. If hands-on preparation isn't your thing, use a knife and chop the meat into fine bits.

- The grain on **beef brisket** runs in two directions, so separate the cuts before you slice the meat. Carve on the bias across the grain into thin slices no thicker than a pencil. Figure 4-5 shows you how to slice brisket — an extra-critical point given the texture of brisket.

- For **pulled chicken,** dig into the cooled bird with hands or forks, tearing the meat from the bones. Of course, you can also serve the whole pieces.

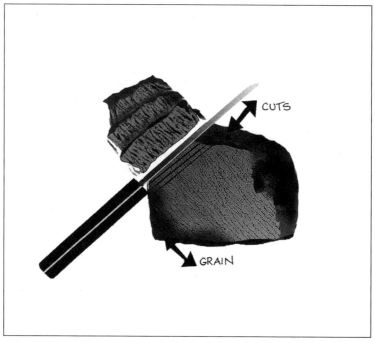

Figure 4-5: Cutting across brisket's grain is important for getting the most appealing texture.

Part II

Preparation Prevails: Using Rubs and Marinades

The 5th Wave   By Rich Tennant

"This is a wonderful rub. We use it on everything — fish, chicken, calluses..."

In this part . . .

*P*at on a rub or soak meat in marinade and magic happens. Rubs season and tenderize meat, help seal
in moisture while you cook, and impart a crisp crust.
Marinades infuse meat with flavor, adding not just interest
but tenderness. In this part, you find out how to use rubs
and marinades and how to mix up batches of either by
using the ample recipes or instructions for building
your own.

Chapter 5

Mixing and Matching in Rubs and Marinades

In This Chapter

▶ Creating a rub: Four easy pieces

▶ Blending spices in tasty combos

▶ Watching out for clashing flavors

▶ Building marinades from scratch

▶ Creating harmonious combos of meat and marinade

▶ Maximizing your marinades

---

*W*hat you do before you cook meat makes all the difference in the result you get. No pressure, but really, taking the time to let meat sit in a dry rub or marinade gives the stuff flavor and can even bring any meat extra juiciness and more toothsome texture.

Dry rubs and marinades overlap in function but operate very differently. In most cases, you use one or the other. This chapter gives you the goods on what dry rubs and marinades do and how they do it. You also find an overview of what goes into dry rubs and marinades. They have many, many permutations, but the basic formula for either is significantly easier than pie.

Building a Dry Rub from the Binder Up

A dry rub creates a bark on the outside of whatever meat you're cooking, and that bark holds in the moisture. Put it together well, and the rub that builds the bark also provides some incredible flavor in the meat.

You find as many recipes for rub as there are cooks, and there's no end to the possibilities. There is, however, a basic formula for building a rub. (And, really, a limited number of standard combinations that survive because they work so well together. The difference in these lies in the proportions of ingredients, and playing with proportions could keep a cook busy ad infinitum.) The following breakdown describes how most dry rubs come together:

- ✔ **Binder:** Something relatively neutral that provides a base for all the other flavors. Paprika is a commonly used binder for traditional barbecue dry rubs; cumin shows up in a lot of Indian rubs; and if you're following a Jamaican recipe, brown sugar is likely to fill this role. (But brown sugar is not really dry, and because it's not powdery, it tends to sit on the meat instead of penetrating it to add flavor.)

- ✔ **Salt:** Plain old table salt, sea salt, or kosher — garlic, even — you want some kind of salt in the mix for flavor, texture, and its tenderizing effect. A little salt draws out other flavors in your rub — but use too much, and all you taste is salt.

- ✔ **Sweet:** Sugar adds body and helps balance your dry rub. Plain old granulated sugar does the trick, and you get good results from cane sugar or brown sugar as well. Use sugar sparingly, though; too much will give your meat a burnt and bitter crust. Turn to Chapter 8 to find out more about sugar's problem properties.

- ✔ **Power:** You generally add one or two strong flavors to give your rub oomph: spices like chili powder, curry powder, cayenne pepper, or crushed dried chilies work beautifully.

The four elements in the preceding list get you started, and then you add some of this, a little of that, until you find the flavor you're looking for. Grab some dry mustard; toss in granulated onion — whatever sounds tasty, within reason. In the upcoming section, "Warring Flavors You Don't Want to Mix," I steer you away from some bad ideas regarding spice mixing.

When you start putting together a rub, determine the main flavor you want to come through, and then make sure you give that flavor top billing. Use equal amounts of sugar and salt, for example, and you end up tasting neither. But if you want a sweet rub and use more sugar than salt, you get sweetness with salt flavor that keeps the rub in balance.

Smelling the flavor

"Eye appeal is half the meal" is a mantra that reverberates through restaurants, where presentation is critical. At competitions, barbecue cooks go to great lengths to make sure their food looks lovely, even spraying it with apple juice to give it an eye-catching sheen. Turns out, the nose has much more to do with your perception of taste than your eyes.

The tongue picks up on only five different flavors (sweet, sour, bitter, pungent, and salty), but the nose can discern among thousands of aromas. Molecules from herbs and spices are highly volatile and so fly up into the air and into your nose, bringing the aroma of the seasoning with them. Even as you're chewing, the aroma-containing molecules are meandering into your nasal cavity. The sensation of smelling mingles with that of tasting, and the whole glorious combination comes together as pleasure (or not).

You get a first-hand, um, taste of this phenomenon when you have a cold and can't get a good whiff of your food. Those clogged sinuses of yours are the reason you can't taste the difference between an apple and a raw potato.

 Rubs work best when they're composed of fine powders that give you an even coat on the meat. And fresh-ground herbs release more flavor than those that have been ground months before. A coffee grinder works great for reducing coarse salt, coriander seeds, or pretty much anything else to a powder. If you already have a grinder that you use for your morning coffee, get a second one just for grinding seasonings; otherwise, you're likely to end up with some funky-tasting coffee.

And speaking of coffee — many cooks use it in their rubs. Ground coffee (but not used coffee grounds) gives a unique flavor to meat and is a good complement to smoking. Legend has it, the notion of using coffee grounds came as an accident when a cook spilled some coffee on the cutting board where his waiting steaks sat and decided to roll with it, rolling his steaks in the stuff to tasty effect.

 After you mix any dry rub, seal it in an airtight container and store it at room temperature for about a day. You can skip this step if you're in a hurry, but a nice amalgamating effect comes from letting the spices mingle, making the whole much bigger than the sum of its parts.

Seasonings That Play Well Together

The grains filling little jars in your spice rack started out as weapons. Plants' intense flavors are how they convince animals to get away after taking a bite. Dilution and mixing make the flavors palatable to people, but strike upon the wrong formula of flavors, and your cooking may become noxious in a new way. That doesn't mean you shouldn't experiment, but it does mean that smart experimentation follows a few rules.

As you flip through the recipes in Chapter 6, you probably start to notice a few similarities among them. That's because there's a basic formula for making rubs, and some general guidelines for using seasonings that are never going to change. Don't think for a minute that those truths are limiting factors, though: Within them are at least a gazillion ways to get from spice rack to dry rub. And, as you get a feel for mixing dry rubs, you're likely to want to try your own. This section gives you the basics you need for doing it yourself.

You have centuries of cooking with herbs and spices to draw on, which means a lot of the trial and error of spice pairing has been done for you. Still, no hard and fast rules exist when it comes to putting seasonings together, and your personal palate has a lot to do with the combinations you favor.

 Put every color in a paint box together, and muddy brown is the likely result. Go overboard when putting spices together, and flavors start canceling each other out, leaving you with a tasteless sludge. Keeping your combos simple usually gives you the best-tasting rub.

The following guidelines help you experiment with seasonings without arriving at less-than-toothsome results:

- ✔ Open the lids of the seasonings you plan to use, and set the containers out in a close configuration on the counter. Take a whiff of the melded flavors and see whether anything sticks out as not meshing. Forget that seasoning this time.

- ✔ Use different quantities of spices that have similar qualities. That is, if you're using two sweet spices, like allspice and anise, use a little more of one than the other.

✔ Keep in mind that more is almost never better. Using a few well-matched seasonings usually is preferable to adding and adding and adding flavors.

✔ Shoot for contrast: If you're using a hot spice like cayenne pepper, tone it down with a little sugar.

✔ Remember that the benefit of using some moderately flavored seasonings is that they bind more intense flavors without muddying up the mix. Good choices for this effect are coriander, fennel, paprika, and turmeric.

Table 5-1 shows you time-tested combinations of herbs and spices used for various types of cuisines. Getting a sense of how flavors work together goes a long way toward success as you start experimenting in the kitchen.

Table 5-1	Common Spice Mixes
Spice Mix	*Ingredients*
Chili powder	Allspice, cumin, garlic, onion, oregano, salt
Chinese five-spice powder	Cinnamon, cloves, Szechuan pepper, fennel, star anise
Creole seasoning	Basil, black pepper, cayenne pepper, garlic, onion, oregano, paprika, salt, thyme
Curry powder	Black peppercorns, coriander, fenugreek, ginger, mustard seed, turmeric, red chiles
Garam masala	Bay leaves, black peppercorns, cardamom, cloves, coriander, cumin, ginger, nutmeg
Herbes de Provence	Basil, fennel, lavender, marjoram, rosemary, thyme
Jamaican jerk seasoning	Allspice, chiles, cinnamon, cloves, garlic, ginger, thyme
Pickling spice	Allspice, bay leaves, black peppercorns, cinnamon, cloves, dill seed, ginger, mace, red pepper flakes, yellow mustard seed
Poultry seasoning	Marjoram, oregano, sage, thyme

Mixing Marinades

Part tenderizer, part juicifier, and part *sweet sassy molassey!,* marinades give meat greater toothsomeness in every sense of the word.

A *marinade* is any combination of oil, acid, and herbs that meat soaks in before you cook it. You have an infinite variety of combinations for creating delectable marinades, and with the slightest smarts about how the elements work together, you can whip up versions for any meat you want to cook and any result you want to chow down on.

In this section, you find out how to put together balanced marinades that tenderize, give great pep, and add moisture to whatever meats you may cook. You accomplish that tripartite mission with three kinds of ingredients that vary according to the effect you want to achieve and the kind of meat you're cooking.

Acid

Acids act on proteins in meat, helping them break down and become more tender. As the proteins break down, they leave space within the meat for flavor and moisture to seep in. Acids that commonly are used in marinades include the following:

- ✔ Beer
- ✔ Bourbon or other hard liquors
- ✔ Buttermilk
- ✔ Carbonated beverages (except diet soda, which adds an unpleasant bitter flavor)
- ✔ Coffee
- ✔ Cranberry juice
- ✔ Grapefruit juice
- ✔ Lemon juice
- ✔ Lime juice
- ✔ Orange juice
- ✔ Vinegar
- ✔ Wine
- ✔ Yogurt

Ceviche: The crossroads of marinating and cooking

Travel to South America or Central America, and you probably sample a cold seafood salad called *ceviche*. To make it, bite-size pieces of fish are soaked in lime juice or lemon juice, minced onions and peppers, and maybe cilantro or parsley. Sometimes other minced ingredients, like celery, avocado, or tomato, are added as well. All kinds of fish end up in ceviche, and what kind you find depends in part on where you are.

The acid in the lemon juice or lime juice "cooks" the fish over the course of a couple hours by changing the composition of its proteins, just as heat does, but more gently. Preparing fish this way is gentler than heating it, so the result is more delicately flavored, more succulent fish.

Just like *barbecue,* the word *ceviche* (and the stuff itself) has origins that spark debate. One theory that seems reasonable enough has it stemming from the Iberian Spanish word *escabeche* (meaning "marinade").

 Which works best? Surprisingly, it's the buttermilk and yogurt, which seem to be able to better penetrate meat but without leaving it too tough or mushy-textured. The theory goes that dairy products work best, in part, because they're on the low side of the acid spectrum.

Oil

A marinade's oil is its moisture. A good dose of oil — just about any kind will do — helps meat hang onto whatever moisture it has and even adds to it.

Seasonings

You add flavor with the oil and acid, but you get most of your marinade's *pow* when you use seasonings to build a balanced and interesting combination of flavors. (The earlier section, "Seasonings That Play Well Together," tells you more about how to combine seasonings.)

Matching Marinade to Meat

Many of the same ingredients work no matter what meat you plan to cook: Garlic, black pepper, citrus juice, and ginger are practically ubiquitous marinade ingredients that complement just about anything you could think to cook. Other ingredients work better with particular types of meats.

In this section, I give you some ideas about what works with some of the common meats for outdoor cooking.

Starters for seafood

Because seafood soaks up flavor so quickly, marinades work best when they're subtle, and the type of fish you plan to cook affects the flavors that you use: The stronger flavors that may work for denser, fattier fish like tuna or salmon don't necessarily complement delicate red snapper. And then there's shellfish. Shrimp are great for grilling and can hang with most marinades; scallops need a sure hand for appropriate marinating.

How does all this add up? Here are a few guidelines for marinating fish:

- **Marinate with reserve.** Too much time or intensity enables a marinade to overpower a fish or even cook it (which is tasty, sure, but a whole different animal from marinated, grilled fish).

- **Match subtler flavors to more delicate fish.** The fat content gives you an indication of the fish's muscle in the face of marinade. Fattier fish can withstand stronger flavors than lower-fat fish. If you're cooking tuna or mackerel, for example, you can let loose with some soy sauce, crushed red pepper, wasabi powder, or similarly strong ingredients.

- **Use the tried and true.** Citrus juices and olive oil are always a safe start for fish; black or white pepper, paprika, or a smidge of crushed red pepper can finish the job with surprisingly delicious results that belie the simplicity of the concoction.

Adding oomph to chicken

Chicken is practically a blank canvas and does fine with whatever you choose to paint on it, be that a subtle lemon-herb marinade or an intense chile-ginger version. It's hard to go wrong in part because chicken itself is mildly flavored and its texture makes it somewhat resistant to the seasonings you add (except for the dark meat, which is less dense and picks up flavor more efficiently). Citrus juices, wine, mustard, and soy sauce top a long list of good pairings for chicken.

Because chicken can be resistant to marinade, reserve some of yours (a portion that hasn't touched the raw chicken, of course) to serve with your cooked chicken. You can also boil the marinade (in which case, you can even use leftovers from the marinade bowl) for several minutes to reduce it and create an extra-flavorful sauce for topping or dipping the chicken. An extra dash of the flavors you cooked the chicken in goes a long way toward driving home the result you want.

Good ideas for pork

Pork has a mild flavor that you can easily take in several directions with marinade, and it gives itself over well to the marinade, readily absorbing the flavors. Soy sauce is a stellar starter for pork and shows up in the majority of pork marinade recipes; use it with ginger, garlic, and honey or sugar, and you get a tender, tasty result. Go in the other direction and pair it with fruit juices for a sweeter and milder result.

Pork also does well with delicate, wine-based marinades, and it can stand up to powerful marinades with chile sauce or chipotle peppers.

Do your worst; pork can probably take it.

Sure bets for beef

The rich flavor of beef merits complex flavors in a marinade. Red wine or red wine vinegar are excellent choices, and soy sauce works well, too. Horseradish is a sure bet, and so are Worcestershire sauce, garlic, dry mustard, and ginger.

Herb-wise, thyme or rosemary are great choices; a bay leaf can add the smidge of bitterness that balances meat's savoriness.

Use only a little citrus, if you use it at all. A hint of it can make your other flavors pop, but if the citrus takes over, it clashes with the beef.

Timing Meat's Marinade Soak

The reason different types of meat have different flavors (the structure of their proteins) is the same reason meats handle marinades differently. Leave fish too long in marinade, and you cook it. Denser red meat can take much more time to soak in the flavors of a marinade, but it turns mushy on its edges and tough in the middle if it spends more than the optimal amount of time soaking.

 Use a glass or stainless steel container to marinate meats, or put the meat and the marinade in a plastic freezer bag with a zipper seal. When you use aluminum bowls, the meat picks up unsavory flavors and takes on an unnatural color because the acids in the marinade oxidize molecules in the bowl.

The line between flavorful and over-marinated isn't a thin one. You usually have an unintimidating and wide margin of error to work with. Here are some guidelines for determining the time particular meats need in marinades:

- ✔ **Fish:** Up to an hour
- ✔ **Chicken:** One to three hours
- ✔ **Pork:** Four to seven hours
- ✔ **Lamb:** Five to eight hours
- ✔ **Beef:** Big barbecue cuts (like brisket), 12 to 24 hours; smaller cuts that you grill, 6 to 12 hours

The timing depends somewhat on the flavors in the marinade, as well. If you're using a subtle marinade, go for the longer side of the timing window; for intense marinades, err on the side of caution.

 If you're marinating meat for more than an hour, do so in the fridge. You don't want to risk giving bacteria a place to grow. Those opportunistic suckers are lurking and ready to multiply like crazy. Make sure you throw out any leftover marinade for that very reason. Juices from the raw meat that soaked in it are an easy target for a bacteria infestation.

Chapter 6

Crafting Dry Rubs for Any Meat or Taste

A little sweet, some salt, and some heat, if that's what you're into — just about any combination of flavors can go into a tasty barbecue rub.

Some seasonings are barbecue staples. (Watch for garlic and onion powders, paprika, and cayenne in several of the recipes to come.) and others break the traditional mold. Some cooks throw in practically the whole spice cabinet, and others keep things simple with just a handful of ingredients and get results just as good.

Using a dry rub is exceptionally easy. Just sprinkle your mix onto the meat you plan to cook and then pat it or rub it lightly into the surface so that it really sticks.

After you introduce rub to meat, wrap the meat in plastic and let it sit in the fridge for a while so the rub gets a chance to do its work. You can get away with skipping this step and going right to the cooking part of the program. Because the rub actually sits right on the meat, you're not going to lose flavor as you would if you were to pull a meat from marinade before its time.

If you're concerned about fat in your diet, you may be pleased to know that, unlike marinades, dry rubs add flavor without using oil or any other fat. Of course, they're made up of a lot of sugar and salt, so they don't exactly qualify as health food.

You can store a dry rub for about six months if you keep it in an airtight container and away from light.

Have fun getting your feet wet with the recipes in this chapter. Chances are good that you'll soon be drawing raves for your own unique seasoning blends.

Combining Flavors for Classic Dry Rubs

Salt and sugar are almost givens for a rub (although the upcoming section, "Bucking Tradition with Rubs Exotic and Inventive" includes a no-salt version); what you do otherwise is up to you. Still, certain flavors have been working their way into dry rubs for decades, and in this section you find recipes that draw from barbecue tradition.

Smokey Joel's Competition BBQ Rub

Smokey Joel (also known as Joel Schwabe) fares well with this rub in competitions.

Preparation time: *5 minutes*

Cooking time: *None*

Yield: *About 1 cup*

¼ cup brown sugar

¼ cup paprika

¼ tablespoon kosher salt

1 tablespoon granulated garlic

1 tablespoon onion powder

1 teaspoon cayenne pepper

1 teaspoon chili powder

1 teaspoon black pepper

1½ teaspoons dried oregano

1½ teaspoons cumin

1½ teaspoons celery salt

1 tablespoon dried, grated lemon or orange peel (optional)

In a large bowl, combine all ingredients and mix well.

Smoke Hunters' BBQ Rub

The Smoke Hunters team advises using this rub, which is the one they took to their early competitions, on pork ribs, pork shoulder, or chicken. The recipe, as written, produces about 2 cups of rub, which may be overkill if you don't use it regularly. Cut the recipe in half, and you still have enough for a good 15 pounds of meat.

Preparation time: *5 minutes*

Cooking time: *None*

Yield: *About 2 cups*

½ cup brown sugar

½ cup Sugar In The Raw

½ cup paprika

6 tablespoons fresh ground black pepper

6 tablespoons kosher salt

1 ½ tablespoons granulated garlic

1 ½ tablespoons granulated onion

2 teaspoons cayenne pepper

In a large bowl, combine all ingredients and mix well.

Sugar In The Raw is the brand name of turbinado sugar, which isn't refined as white sugar is and so still has some of the flavor and nutrients from the sugar cane juice. It has a natural brown color and larger crystals than refined white sugar, but you can use it in much the same way when it comes to sweetening coffee or cereal.

Turbinado has more moisture than white sugar. In flavor and texture, it's somewhere in the middle of brown and white sugars. It's more likely to replace brown sugar in recipes than white because of its moisture content, and it also will harden as brown sugar does if it's not stored in an airtight container.

Pirate Potion #4

This recipe comes from the Pirates of the Grill, who warn that it's a spicy one but has a lot of depth. Fred Larsen from the team says the rub was developed to use on pork but that it's a swell seasoning for your morning eggs, too.

Preparation time: *5 minutes*

Cooking time: *None*

Yield: *About 3 cups*

1 cup brown sugar	1 tablespoon chipotle pepper
1 cup salt	1 tablespoon white pepper
½ cup paprika	1 teaspoon jalapeño pepper
¼ cup chili powder	¼ cup garlic powder
⅛ cup black pepper	1 tablespoon cumin
1 tablespoon cayenne pepper	1 teaspoon onion powder

In a large bowl, combine all ingredients and mix well.

Vary It! *Try using seasoned salt rather than plain table salt.*

Paradise Jerk Rub

The Pig Smokers in Paradise BBQ Team earns kudos when it uses this jerk rub on pork: "It goes well with about any type of pork cut," says member Connie Owens.

Preparation time: *5 minutes*

Cooking time: *None*

Yield: *About 1 cup*

6 tablespoons onion powder	2 tablespoons granulated sugar
6 tablespoons onion flakes	4 ½ teaspoons dried thyme
2 tablespoons ground allspice	4 ½ teaspoons cinnamon
2 tablespoons black pepper	1½ teaspoons nutmeg
2 tablespoons cayenne pepper	1½ teaspoons ground cloves

In a large bowl, combine all ingredients and mix well.

Spicy Rub #1 for Beef

John Webb, from the Up-in-Smoke team, said he started making spicy rubs because he had a sinus infection that interfered with his taste buds. "I started adding more and more spice until I could taste something," he said. "The downside was that everyone else was tasting the meat and saying, 'Wow — that is way too spicy, but pretty good.' I learned from that experience and cut down on the spices until I got the right blend. They still say, 'Wow,' but now they follow that with, 'Boy, that's good.'"

Webb makes his rub in big batches, using whole 3-ounce bottles, but he says that the point is that you use equal parts of each ingredient (except the cayenne powder or black pepper).

Preparation time: *10 minutes*

Cooking time: *None*

Yield: *About 4 cups*

3 ounces paprika	*3 ounces garlic flakes*
3 ounces cumin	*3 ounces onion flakes*
3 ounces Cajun spice	*3 ounces natural cane sugar*
3 ounces garlic powder	*1 tablespoon cayenne powder or black pepper*

1 Combine all ingredients in a food processor.

2 Grind the mixture about 10 seconds.

Variation: *To use this rub with chicken or pork, add 1 tablespoon mustard powder.*

 You can add further dimension to any dry rub by adding just enough liquid to turn it into a paste or *wet rub*. Any flavorful liquid will do the trick, but some of the favorites are

- Apple juice
- Beer
- Mustard
- Olive oil
- Orange juice
- Worcestershire sauce
- Yogurt

Shigs-in-Pit Bootheel Butt Rub

Todd Grantham of the Shigs-in-Pit BBQ team said the name of this rub (and the team's sauce in Chapter 9) came from the area two of his team members hail from — the Bootheel area of southeast Missouri. He says that rubs of this style are popular in restaurants in that area.

Grantham advises using the rub on all things pork, especially ribs and pork butt. The heavy yield of this recipe means that you may want to cut it in half. Doing so still yields enough rub for two healthy-sized meals.

Preparation time: *5 minutes*

Cooking time: *None*

Yield: *About 2 cups*

¼ cup kosher salt

¼ cup Accent (monosodium glutamate, or MSG)

½ cup granulated sugar

½ cup light brown sugar

½ cup fine organic cane sugar (turbinado)

1 tablespoon granulated garlic

1½ tablespoons granulated onion

2 tablespoons paprika

2 tablespoons chili powder

2 tablespoons ground black pepper

1½ tablespoons ground cayenne pepper

1 tablespoon thyme

1 tablespoon ground cumin

1 teaspoon ground nutmeg

1½ tablespoons cinnamon

1 teaspoon hickory smoke salt

1 teaspoon celery salt

In a large bowl, combine all ingredients and mix well.

A pinch of salt facts

No barbecue rub is complete without salt, and neither is any diet. Not only does salt intensify aromas and flavors in the food that you use it on but it fills a physical need in the human body. Among other things, sodium keeps nerve impulses flowing and chloride helps keep your digestive system in top form. (Of course, the amount of salt most people eat far surpasses the single gram per day that is necessary to get the balancing job done.)

Salt comes from oceans and either is dried directly from the water and dubbed *sea salt* or mined from seas that dried up and left behind massive salty deposits.

Strangely enough, this essential substance has achieved chichi status in the past few years, and gourmet salt stores selling expensive, rare variations have popped up, as have salt-tasting parties (not events for the high of blood pressure).

Different salts do bring slightly different flavors, and you also can find flavored salts, like the hickory smoke salt that the Shigs-in-Pit Bootheel Rub recipe calls for. No reason not to use a flavored salt in your rub, and doing so can be a shortcut or a way to add flavor that you otherwise wouldn't be able to bring to the rub.

Because it's fine-textured, table salt is a good choice for dry rubs because you don't have to grind it to get it to stick fast to the meat surface. Most seasoned salts also are fine-textured, but they come with a caveat: You lose a degree of control when you use already-combined seasonings. You can be certain of getting exactly the ratio of flavors that you want when you work from scratch.

Everything Rub

Rich Allen of Dick's Bodacious Bar-B-Q, Inc., offers up this recipe that he says can easily strike up a beautiful relationship with any meat you want to cook.

Preparation time: *5 minutes*

Cooking time: *None*

Yield: *About ⅓ cup*

¼ cup seasoning salt

1 tablespoon coarse ground black pepper

1 teaspoon celery salt

1 teaspoon mild chili powder

2 teaspoons garlic powder

In a small bowl, combine all ingredients and mix.

Tip: *Press into meat at least half an hour before you plan to cook it.*

Super Simple Brisket Rub

Doug Spiller of Smoked Signals BBQ keeps things nice and simple with this rub of just four ingredients used in equal parts.

Spiller advises using a can of beer to mop your brisket when you use this rub so that you can keep the flavors moving around on the meat.

In the last half-hour of cooking, Spiller uses three parts Sweet Baby Ray's sauce cut with one part beer to finish the brisket. He says that the sauce is a perfect way to not only cut through some of the heat of the rub but also to give the brisket a nice glaze.

Preparation time: *5 minutes*

Cooking time: *None*

Yield: *1 cup*

¼ cup black pepper

¼ cup salt

¼ cup paprika

¼ cup onion powder

In a large bowl, combine all ingredients and mix well.

Rib Dust

Rich Allen is a Texan who brought his barbecue to the Midwest when he founded Dick's Bodacious Bar-B-Q, Inc., a string of Indiana restaurants. His rib rub is a well-balanced affair that makes good use of just a few flavors.

Preparation time: *5 minutes*

Cooking time: *None*

Yield: *About 2 cups*

¾ cup paprika

½ cup chili powder

¼ cup cumin

1 teaspoon coarse ground black pepper

¼ cup brown sugar

1 tablespoon thyme

2 tablespoons garlic powder

2 tablespoons onion powder

1 tablespoon salt

In a small bowl, combine all ingredients and mix well.

Tip: *Press into meat at least half an hour before you plan to cook it.*

Pork Perfection

The Smoked Signals BBQ team took home a first-place trophy with this rub, which team leader Doug Spiller said he came up with after much studying of recipes in books.

The rub includes a pretty heavy amount of sugar, and Spiller explains that that's what gives the pork a nice bark.

Preparation time: *5 minutes*

Cooking time: *None*

Yield: *About 1 cup*

¼ cup granulated sugar

¼ cup course cane sugar (turbinado)

3 tablespoons brown sugar

¼ cup kosher salt

¼ cup paprika

1 tablespoon dry mustard

1 tablespoon onion powder

1 tablespoon black pepper

2 teaspoons white pepper

2 teaspoons garlic powder

2 teaspoons chipotle chile powder

1 Combine all ingredients in a food processor.

2 Grind the mixture about 10 seconds.

You want a bark on your barbecued meats not only for the flavors of the seasonings within it but also to hold in the moisture of the meat. Rubs that include a lot of sugar tend to form a heartier bark, but they fare poorly under high heat.

If you're reaching into a bowl to sprinkle rub onto meat, make sure that you don't touch the meat and then put your hand into the rub. Doing so contaminates the rub with the meat juices and invites bacteria. Keep your rub clean, and it'll last several months.

Yard Bird Rub

Rich Allen of Dick's Bodacious Bar-B-Q, Inc., also served as the technical reviewer for this book. Here, he offers a straightforward rub concocted just for chicken and turkey.

Preparation time: *5 minutes*

Cooking time: *None*

Yield: *About ¼ cup rub*

3 tablespoons poultry seasoning

1 teaspoon salt

1 tablespoon coarse ground black pepper

1 tablespoon paprika

1 teaspoon thyme

In a small bowl, combine all ingredients and mix well.

Tip: *Press into meat at least half an hour before you plan to cook it.*

Jamaican Rib Rub

Poppi-Q BBQ founder Tom Schneider likes this spicy rub when it's paired with a citrus-based barbecue sauce. This recipe covers four slabs of pork baby back or spare ribs.

Preparation time: *5 minutes*

Cooking time: *None*

Yield: *About ¾ cup*

½ cup dark brown sugar, packed

2 tablespoons sea salt

1 tablespoon garlic powder

1 tablespoon onion powder

½ teaspoon ground black pepper

½ teaspoon dried and ground thyme

½ teaspoon habenero or scotch bonnet pepper powder

½ teaspoon allspice

½ teaspoon cinnamon

½ teaspoon dried and ground ginger

In a large bowl, combine all ingredients and mix well.

Note: *Make sure you wash your hands after handling the habenero powder. Rubbing your eyes or other delicate regions with the stuff provides a burn you don't want to feel.*

Bucking Tradition with Rubs Exotic and Inventive

Pit masters aren't the only cooks to use combinations of seasonings to improve the flavor and texture of meat. In this section, you find rubs that come from other cultures, as well as rubs that deviate from the barbecue tradition.

Sweet Persian Rub

The Persian Empire influenced a large part of the culinary flavors throughout Asia. This recipe from Brandon Hamilton pays tribute to those wonderful flavors. It goes well with seafood, chicken, lamb, and beef.

Preparation time: *5 minutes*

Cooking time: *None, but let sit at least 2 hours or overnight*

Yield: *About ¾ cup*

1 tablespoon black mustard seeds	*2 tablespoon sesame seeds*
2 tablespoons ground cumin	*2 tablespoons brown sugar*
2 teaspoons turmeric	*2 tablespoons ground coriander*
2 tablespoons kosher salt	*1 tablespoon curry powder*
2 teaspoons cayenne	*2 teaspoons ground ginger*

In a large bowl, combine all ingredients and mix well.

Curry powder, which you use for Brandon Hamilton's Sweet Persian Rub, is a catchall term for spice mixes that mimic the combination of seasonings used in Indian curry sauces. They're made up of a host of other roasted and powdered seasonings that varies according to who made the mix. Curry powder usually contains at least a dozen seasonings, which contribute to its complex flavor.

Curry powders are usually available in the grocery store, but you may find a better selection if you turn to a specialty market or to the Internet. The Spice House (www.thespicehouse.com) is a good source with several varieties for sale.

Zesty No-Salt Herbal BBQ Rub

Paul Kirk offers a unique, salt-free rub that gets a spicy punch from a goodly dose of chili powder.

Preparation time: *5 minutes*

Cooking time: *None*

Yield: *About 2 cups*

1 cup cane sugar	1 tablespoon granulated onion
½ cup light brown sugar	1 teaspoon basil
¼ cup chili powder	1 teaspoon marjoram
3 tablespoons fine ground black pepper	1 teaspoon dried mustard
1 teaspoon cayenne pepper	1 teaspoon parsley
1 tablespoon dill weed	1 teaspoon crushed rosemary leaves
1 tablespoon granulated garlic	1 teaspoon rubbed sage

In a large bowl, combine all ingredients and mix well.

Grilled Leg of Lamb Seasoning

Paul Kirk says his recipe for leg-of-lamb seasoning covers up to 5 pounds of trimmed and butterflied lamb.

Preparation time: *5 minutes*

Cooking time: *None*

Yield: *About ¾ cup seasoning*

¼ cup coarse ground black pepper	1 tablespoon crushed rosemary leaves
3 tablespoons kosher salt	½ cup balsamic vinegar
2 tablespoons dried flaked garlic	

In a small bowl, combine all ingredients and mix well.

Note: *Store in refrigerator in airtight container or apply directly to lamb, using a pastry brush to paint it onto the meat.*

Lemon Rub a Dub Dub

Team N2Que calls its Lemon Rub a Dub Dub mix a great match for fish and chicken.

Preparation time: *5 minutes*

Cooking time: *None*

Yield: *2 tablespoons*

4 teaspoons lemon pepper

2 teaspoons garlic powder

2 teaspoons oregano

2 teaspoons thyme

½ teaspoon salt

In a small bowl, combine all ingredients and mix well.

Fish is a lot more delicate than pork, chicken, or pretty much anything else you may cook. When you apply rub to fish, you're better off just sprinkling it over the top instead of patting it on or rubbing it into the flesh. And because fish so easily picks up flavors, you use less of the rub than you do when you're putting it on meats.

If you're using a rub on chicken, make sure to pull back the skin and sprinkle the rub directly onto the meat.

Chapter 7

Mixing Tried-and-True Marinades

In This Chapter

▶ Finding time-tested ways to add flavor

▶ Concocting toothsome mixtures for your barbecue

▶ Bringing extra oomph to whatever you cook

A little acidity, some seasonings, maybe some chiles, and some time turn your meals into something entirely different, taking meat up several levels in flavor and juiciness.

You don't need too much time to get the great results that marinades give, just a little planning so you can ensure that you give meat plenty of time to soak up the flavor before you cook it. Cut that short, and you lose the effect.

In this chapter, you find marinades of all kinds and for most meats from barbecue cooks who've tested variation after variation before hitting on their masterpieces. They've done the work so all you have to do is some mixing and refrigerating and collecting of compliments.

Priming Pork or Poultry

Dark or white and other white, chicken and pork don't offer a lot in the way of strong flavor on their own, but they both take to flavors you add like a teenage girl to sarcasm. You don't have much to worry about when it comes to marinade flavors clashing with the mild meat, so chicken and pork make good media for experimentation.

Chapter 5 gives you points to consider when mixing up your own marinades from scratch.

Cooking whole chickens or turkeys often presents a problem because the two kinds of meat (white and dark) have very different makeups, the dark legs being more rife with connective tissue that can make meat chewy. Using a brine or marinade to weaken that connective tissue helps you get a more even texture across the two types of meat. But your best bet is to cut the chicken apart so that you can cook the legs and breast separately.

Plumping a bird or chop with brine

When you use a brine, the meat you cook stays plumper than un-brined meat does. That's because brine makes use of salt to wreak tasty havoc on the muscle fibers of meat. One element of that result is opening up the muscle fibers to the liquid in the brine; another is preventing the muscle fibers from reconnecting when cooking is done. Both components make for juicier, more tender meat.

Brines typically get about 5 percent of their total weight from salt. Many brine recipes, including Charlie's, account for what would otherwise be overwhelming saltiness in the finished product by adding sugar. Experiment with honey, molasses, or brown sugar to impart further flavor while you combat the salt.

Rinse off any brine you use before you cook the meat, unless you enjoy digging into a salt lick on your plate.

Charlie's Pork Brine

Charlie Lamb of Charlie's Butcher Block used early competitions to hone his barbecue skills, picking the brains of fellow cooks but says that getting your hands dirty is the best way to progress: "The more you do it, the better you get — as long as you learn from your mistakes," he said. "Experiment, and don't get discouraged." His brine recipe is simplicity defined, belying its delicious effect.

Preparation time: *5 minutes*

Cooking time: *About 10 minutes, plus time to cool*

Yield: *3 quarts*

3 quarts water

¾ cup kosher salt

½ cup plus 2 tablespoons sugar

1 In a large stock pot, combine all ingredients and mix.

2 Bring to a boil.

3 Remove from heat and let cool.

4 Add pork, and brine in the refrigerator for as long as 24 hours.

Variation: *Charlie says that you can add any flavor you like to turn this brine into a marinade. He recommends fresh garlic and black peppercorns but encourages you to get creative.*

 Make sure that whenever you brine meat, you do so in the refrigerator or in a cooler. You want to make sure the temperature of the brine and the meat stays below 40 degrees.

Poultry and Pork Brine

The KRE Smokers team uses this recipe for whole turkey or chicken, and the team smokes it with pecan and hickory, and then a little cherry wood to give the bird color at the end.

Preparation time: *5 minutes*

Cooking time: *20 minutes*

Yield: *About 1 gallon*

10 cups apple juice	*¼ cup sugar*
6 cups water	*¼ cup brown sugar*
1 cup coarse kosher salt	

1 In a large pot, combine all ingredients and mix.

2 Warm over low heat until sugars and salt dissolve.

3 Let cool in refrigerator until cold.

4 Add meat and brine (12 to 14 hours for turkey or pork loin, less for smaller meats).

5 After marinating, rinse brine off meat before cooking or adding other seasonings.

Many of the meats you find in grocery stores have been "enhanced" with a solution that's much like a brine. Manufacturers inject a mix of water, salt, and sodium phosphate to do basically the same thing you do at home with a brine. The theory is just the same: The salt opens up space within the proteins for the water to hang out and keep the meat moist. The sodium phosphate helps the meat hold onto the added water. Enhanced meats may also contain compounds that inhibit bacteria from growing.

Enhanced meat isn't necessarily bad (although it does obviously contain a lot more sodium than meat alone), but it makes your job harder. With all those added elements, you have less control over the end result of your cooking. Did you oversalt your dry rub or was all that salt in the chicken already?

The U.S. Food and Drug Administration requires that any enhanced meat is clearly labeled. Keep an eye out for fine print that includes words like *marinated, injected,* or *enhanced.*

Finding formulas for marinades

Marinades hold a lot of power but unfortunately don't reach the magic status that some people attribute to them. Meat is mostly water to begin with, and flavor itself is fat soluble instead of water soluble, meaning that the two aren't exactly a match made in meat heaven. Even so, soaking a meat in marinade does a lot to impart flavor, and the acid in a marinade works to tenderize the meat. (Chapter 5 tells you more about the process.)

Rub and Marinade for Eight-Bone Pork Roast

The results of this pork roast are impressive enough that the simplicity of Paul Kirk's recipe is a surprise.

Preparation time: *10 minutes*

Cooking time: *45 minutes*

Yield: *½ cup rub and 1 roast (about 6 to 8 servings)*

¼ cup unsalted butter, softened

2 tablespoons red port wine

2 tablespoons cane syrup

2 tablespoons muscadine jelly

¼ cup minced garlic

1 tablespoon chopped fresh tarragon

1 tablespoon chopped fresh thyme

1 tablespoon chopped fresh basil

1 tablespoon chopped fresh rosemary

1 teaspoon salt

1 teaspoon pepper

1 cup chicken broth

1 roast, about 6 to 8 pounds

1 In a small bowl, combine the butter, port, syrup, and jelly.

2 Spread mixture over roast.

3 In a second small bowl, combine the remaining ingredients.

4 Add the broth to the roasting pan for grill or smoker.

5 Cook at 350 degrees for 45 minutes or until internal temperature reaches 145 degrees for medium rare.

A thick-skinned wild grape that grows best in hot, humid climates, muscadines have a delicate, sweet flavor. Muscadines have black or purple skin, unless they're scuppernogs, a greenish-bronze-skinned variety of muscadine. You find them growing primarily in the southeastern United States, where they've become a favorite of jelly makers. Live elsewhere? You can most likely find muscadine jelly (or syrup, or even wine) in gourmet shops or order it online.

The basil breakdown

Maybe the best remnant of the disco era, basil started taking hold in American cooking late in the 1970s and has since become almost a staple, trickling down from fine dining to even fast-food restaurants. It got a late start in the United States, but it's been around for thousands of years and a part of many cuisines during that time.

Basil is an aromatic herb and shows up in endless varieties, but the one you most commonly find in the grocery store is sweet basil. Even that may taste very different (bringing flavors as diverse as lime and cinnamon) depending on where and how it's grown.

Hindus include a particular species of basil — *Ocimum sanctum,* also called tulsi or holy basil — in their religious practice and use it as a remedy for insect bites, colds, stress, and a host of other ailments.

Basil is an easy plant to grow. A single plant can produce more than a family can handle during the course of a summer, and it flourishes inside as well. Good thing, because, like many fresh herbs, basil can cost a mint at the grocery.

Garlic Basil Chicken Marinade

Garlic cloves and fresh basil add discernable but not overpowering flavor to Paul Kirk's chicken marinade.

Preparation time: *10 minutes*

Cooking time: *None*

Yield: *1½ cups*

½ cup white wine vinegar

¼ cup fresh lemon juice

¼ cup distilled water

8 fresh basil leaves

4 large garlic cloves

1 teaspoon sea salt

1 teaspoon fresh ground black pepper

½ cup canola oil

1 In food processor, combine vinegar, lemon juice, water, basil, garlic, sea salt, and black pepper.

2 Process, slowly adding oil in a steady stream. Store in refrigerator in airtight container.

Prepping Beef and Lamb with Flavors That Blare or Whisper

Beef and lamb tend to have some intense flavors right out of the gate. You can work with a marinade to override those by applying intense flavors or give them just a complement of soft marinade flavors.

Cajun Marinade for Grilled Beef Tenderloin

Paul Kirk puts *beef tenderloin* right in the name of this recipe, but you have no reason not to use it on any old steak you may want to throw on the grill. Kirk's recipe makes enough marinade for about 4 to 6 pounds of beef.

Preparation time: *10 minutes*

Cooking time: *2 to 8 hours of marinade time*

Yield: *¾ cup marinade*

¼ cup Louisiana hot sauce

¼ cup teriyaki sauce

2 tablespoons Worcestershire sauce

2 garlic cloves, pressed

1 tablespoon Creole or Cajun seasoning

1 In a small bowl, combine all ingredients.

2 Refrigerate or use right away.

Vietnamese Lemongrass Rub

This recipe from Brandon Hamilton creates a *wet rub* — any seasoning mix that incorporates a little oil to form a paste. The lemongrass offers a nice summery flavor that pairs especially well with lamb. You can use this rub with seafood or chicken, too.

Preparation time: *20 minutes*

Cooking time: *None.*

Yield: *4 servings*

3 fresh lemongrass stalks, root end trimmed and 1 or 2 outer leaves discarded from each stalk

2 shallots, chopped

3 garlic cloves, chopped

2 teaspoons freshly chopped and peeled ginger

Zest of 1 lemon

Juice of 1 lime

1½ tablespoons sugar

1 teaspoon salt

½ teaspoon ground cayenne pepper

3 tablespoons water

2 tablespoons fish sauce (optional)

5 tablespoons peanut oil or vegetable oil

1 Thinly slice bottom 6 inches of the lemongrass, discarding the remainder.

2 Puree lemongrass, shallots, garlic, ginger, lemon zest, lime juice, sugar, salt, cayenne, water, and fish sauce in a food processor, scraping down the sides occasionally, until as smooth as possible, about 2 minutes.

3 To finish the rub, slowly drizzle the peanut oil or vegetable oil into the rub mixture while the food processor is on. Continue processing until oil is incorporated.

Note: *Use the wet rub just like you would a marinade, letting it sit on the meat in the refrigerator to absorb the flavors. Blot off the wet rub before you cook.*

You can find lemongrass in the produce sections of most grocery stores. It's a perennial grass that has an extremely tough texture but a very fresh and light lemon flavor that is used a lot in Thai and Vietnamese cooking. Look for firm stalks that are pale yellow or white at the bottom and green elsewhere. Leave browned stalks of lemongrass in the store. If you're having trouble finding lemongrass, try an Asian market.

Teriyaki Marinade

This recipe from the Team N2Que works as well with chicken or fish as it does with steak.

Preparation time: *5 minutes*

Cooking time: *None*

Yield: *¼ cup*

1 tablespoon fresh minced ginger	*½ teaspoon dried red pepper flakes*
3 tablespoons soy sauce	*Salt and pepper, to taste*
1 minced shallot	

1 Combine all ingredients in a large freezer bag or plastic bowl with lid and mix.

2 Refrigerate or use right away.

Tip: *See Chapter 5 for advice about marinade times.*

Playing barbecue doctor: Getting marinade down deep with injections

Marinade doesn't exactly invade meat like the Vikings into the British Isles. It just can't find its way into the middle of the meat without a little help. Injecting the marinade into the meat solves the problem, putting the juicy, flavorful marinade right where you want it. Injecting the marinade into the meat cuts down on the time you need to let it sit before cooking because you don't have to wait around for it to mosey into the heart of the meat.

A number of meat injectors are available online and in kitchen stores. They're like extra-big syringes that you draw marinade into and then poke into the meat so that you can slowly push the marinade right into the fibers.

Injecting meat doesn't require any special talent; you don't need to study up on special techniques to get this simple job done. Just make sure to inject the marinade throughout the meat so that you don't end up with concentrations of marinade in some spots and untouched meat in others.

Hot Pepper Steak Marinade

A standby for Team Pepperitaville, this super-spicy marinade works especially well for steak, but it's nice on chicken or pork, too. And just in case you're planning to cook venison, as the team often does, add Italian dressing to the mix.

Preparation time: *45 minutes (including roasting and peeling)*

Cooking time: *20 minutes*

Yield: *About 3 cups*

10 jalapeño peppers	*½ cup vinegar*
5 cayenne peppers	*1 cup water*
1 green bell pepper	*Juice of ½ lime*
2 banana peppers	*1 cup packed brown sugar*
4 Roma tomatoes	*¼ cup granulated sugar*
2 cloves garlic	*¼ cup soy sauce*
1 tablespoon Creole seasoning	*6 ounces tomato paste*

1 Roast jalapeño, cayenne, green bell, and banana peppers (see Chapter 12 for instructions; the oven-roasting method works better for the smaller peppers).

2 Peel and deseed roasted peppers, wearing plastic gloves or washing your hands immediately afterward.

3 Peel tomatoes (see Chapter 12) and garlic.

4 In food processor, process tomatoes and garlic until they're almost smooth.

5 In a medium pot, combine pepper mixture and all other ingredients.

6 Over medium heat, cook mixture until it reaches the consistency you want. (It thickens as it cooks.)

7 Let cool and pour into airtight storage containers.

Note: *A little of this mix goes a long way, but the marinade keeps well in the fridge for a good long time, so this 3-cup batch is likely to last a while.*

Brisket Marinade

Sweet as Coke tastes when you drink it, it offers acidity in recipes like this one, from the GB-Que team.

Preparation time: *5 minutes*

Cooking time: *None, but 8 hours to marinate*

Yield: *About 1¾ cups*

12-ounce can of Coke	*3 tablespoons brown sugar*
¼ cup Worcestershire sauce	*1 tablespoon garlic powder*
2 tablespoons olive oil	*1 teaspoon onion powder*
1 teaspoon ground mustard	*1 tablespoon chipotle pepper flakes*
1 teaspoon cumin	*¼ teaspoon ground cloves*
1 teaspoon ancho chile powder	*Salt and pepper to taste*
1 teaspoon cayenne	*Hot sauce to taste*
1 teaspoon red pepper flakes	

1 In large bowl, mix all ingredients.

2 Use immediately or cover and store in refrigerator.

Hard-working muscles are the hardest to cook to tenderness, and brisket comes in large part from a cow's pectoral muscle, one of the toughest parts of the cow — in both senses of the word.

Turning a tough cut tender is very different from just tossing a New York strip onto the grill. Brisket needs to reach a higher internal temperature than other cuts of beef do before it's at its best. Make sure you bring your brisket to an internal temperature of at least 185 degrees. (See Chapter 4 for more information on target internal temperatures and for the basics about cooking brisket.) Anything less than 185 degrees and you haven't given the collagen enough time to break down. Experiment with cooking brisket even to as high a temperature as 195 degrees as you figure out which method produces the texture you like best.

Mixing Citrus Marinades for Poultry or Shrimp

Mixing lemon, lime, orange, and so on into a marinade is a peachy way to tenderize it. Fresh is preferable because the flavors are more intense when they're coming right out of the fruit instead of out of a container, but using canned or otherwise packaged juice works fine, too.

Lemon Marinade for Smoked Turkey

Raisins add sweetness, and the cilantro and mint leaves give a nice sharp flavor to this marinade by Paul Kirk.

Preparation time: *10 minutes*

Cooking time: *5 minutes*

Yield: *About 1½ cups*

1 cup water	2 tablespoons mint leaves, minced
¼ cup golden raisins	1 teaspoon salt
¼ cup fresh lemon juice	1 teaspoon black pepper
1 tablespoon balsamic vinegar	Zest of one lemon
2 tablespoons cilantro leaves, minced	1 cup olive oil

1 In a small pan, bring the water to a boil.

2 Add the raisins, remove from heat, cover, and let stand 5 minutes.

3 Drain the water from the raisins and combine with remaining ingredients in a medium bowl.

Because you smoke a turkey over such low heat, stuffing becomes a problem. Cooking it on its own, in the oven, works better than cramming it into the bird, an alternative that may not bring the stuffing up to the right temperature. Anyway, smoke flavor doesn't do much for stuffing, so keeping it out of the range of your hickory is preferable by far.

White meat cooks faster than dark meat, and any meat close to the bone is going to be holding a lot more heat than the rest of the bird, so when you test for doneness (a minimum of 165 degrees), make sure your thermometer is hitting the center of the breast. Salmonella is a dark, uncomfortable cloud hanging over your dinner.

Sweet and Sour Orange Marinade for Shrimp

Hot isn't in the title for Paul Kirk's recipe, but you do get the teeniest underscore of heat from the Anaheim chile. Try using a hotter pepper, like jalapeño, if you want further zing.

Preparation time: *5 minutes*

Cooking time: *None*

Yield: *4 servings*

1 Anaheim chile, seeded and minced	2 teaspoons dark sesame oil
3 large garlic cloves, minced	2 teaspoons red wine vinegar
2 teaspoons orange zest	½ teaspoon salt
1 teaspoon peeled, minced ginger	¼ teaspoon sugar
2 tablespoons soy sauce	¼ teaspoon ground Szechuan pepper
2 tablespoons dry sherry	1 pound uncooked shrimp
1 tablespoon hoisin sauce	

1 In a medium bowl, whisk together all ingredients except the shrimp.

2 Add the shrimp to the marinade. Cover and refrigerate an hour or two.

A low- or medium-hot grill does great things for shrimp, which easily pick up charcoal flavor. The little suckers cook in no time, though, so keep a close eye on them and turn them as soon as you see that one side is pink. The second side won't take as much time as the first, so be at the ready with tongs to snatch the shrimp from the heat as soon as both sides have lost their translucence.

Putting a pair of skewers through the shrimp makes them easier to handle, preventing them from rotating on the skewer. Just put two thin skewers about an inch apart through the shrimp to ensure that they don't tear or turn.

Part III
The All-Important Sauce Story

The 5th Wave   By Rich Tennant

"I had the flu when I made up that barbecue sauce. The tang comes from a few squirts of nasal decongestant."

In this part . . .

Ask most people what makes great barbecue, and they tell you it's all in the sauce. (No sauce is going to make desiccated pork butt taste like the food of the gods but, hell, it can cover a few barbecue sins.) In this part, you find out about using sauces and get inspirations for dreaming up your own rave-inducing versions. I give you traditional recipes from all four American barbecue regions and unexpected sauces from all over the world.

Chapter 8

Sorting through the Sauce Story

● ●

In This Chapter

▶ Sizing up the building blocks of sauce

▶ Finding balance for boffo blends

▶ Getting inspiration from unexpected sources

● ●

*L*eave your meat in the smoker too long, and your friends may let you forget it, but present a mundane sauce, and you break what many people consider an unpardonable barbecue sin. (They're right only in part: How well you prepare and cook meat is at least as important as your sauce, but in many minds, sauce is the whole story of barbecue. Can't fight conviction.)

In this part, you find barbecue recipes from all four barbecue regions and some that may hitherto never have been part of American barbecue. But if you really want to get adventurous, run right past the exotic sauces and concoct your own from-scratch barbecue sauce. Doing so is a great party trick because the reality is that it's not as complicated as most people think.

As I tell you in Chapter 4, you use different barbecue sauces at three different stages of preparing your food:

✔ The tomatoey, sugary barbecue sauce that so many people equate with barbecue itself is not a good match for the heat of the grill and tends to burn, so save it for the last few minutes of cooking, brush it on after you've pulled cooked meat from the smoker, or serve it as a dipping sauce.

✔ Sauces made from bases like vinegar and mustard rather than tomato can be used as *mop sauces.* You regularly slather mop sauces on your food as it cooks.

The recipes in this part of the book give you a wide range of sauces not just from around the country but from around the world. In this chapter, I home in on how to create your own traditional barbecue sauce from scratch.

Choosing a Base

The base you use makes up the largest part of your sauce, although it won't necessarily end up being the most notable flavor. Sauce bases set the tone and hold your other ingredients together in a harmonious mix.

Three bases serve as starting block for most of the barbecue sauce that cooks in the United States stake their names on:

- **Mustard:** Sauces that start with mustard run the gamut, showing up in sweet or spicy versions and most often served alongside pork. Mustard and pork bring out the best in each other.

- **Tomato:** Almost synonymous with "barbecue" for many people, tomato-based sauce is the one that fills grocery store shelves and most regularly coats ribs, pulled pork, and so on. Tomatoes are a tangy canvas for sweet sauces and equally at home with sharp, spicy ingredients.

- **Vinegar:** Thin, vinegar-based sauces contain little that's neutral enough to diffuse the strong flavors within them — usually red pepper flakes or pepper sauce, maybe a pinch of sugar. Some add a little tomato or Worcestershire, but vinegar (often apple cider and white vinegars) is responsible for most of the oomph.

Mayonnaise-based "white sauce" is a wild card that originated in Alabama (and has pretty much stayed there, so far). The tart sauce usually includes apple cider vinegar, lemon juice, cayenne pepper, and sugar. You find a recipe for it in Chapter 9.

 Treat white sauce as you would a tomato-based version, keeping it away from heat until the last few minutes of cooking to keep the mayonnaise from separating. You also can use it as a marinade before you get cooking.

White sauce tastes great on chicken, turkey, and pork, and you can use it as a dressing for salads or coleslaw.

Striking a Balance

Despite every successful barbecue cook holding his recipes close to the vest, a basic formula for sauce is no secret at all. Every sauce that works has a balance of sweet, sour, and seasonings. Many throw in heat, too, to keep things interesting.

As you work on your own sauce recipe, effect change step by step. If you mess with too many elements at a time, you can't pin down what's keeping the sauce from working. Change just one part of the recipe for a subsequent batch, and you leave no mystery as to what's making the difference, and then you know better how to proceed toward your masterpiece.

When you start dreaming up your own sauce, keep in mind that you want one element to do most of the work. A sauce needs an identity if it's to become a standout. If you prefer a sweet sauce, let an element like apricot preserves take the stage and give hot elements the role of backup singer. If you want a sour, vinegary sauce, heat and sweet do the doo-wop work.

The following sections run down the common ingredients that go into the various elements of great sauces.

Sweet ideas

Standard granulated sugar works for adding sweetness, sure, but so do a lot of other ingredients, many of which add much more interesting combinations of flavors along with the sweet:

- ✔ Brown sugar
- ✔ Fruit juices (anything from apple to raspberry or pomegranate)
- ✔ Fruit preserves, jams, or jellies
- ✔ Honey
- ✔ Light corn syrup
- ✔ Maple syrup
- ✔ Molasses

The making (and using) of molasses

Molasses isn't necessarily a staple in today's kitchens, but it was the sweetener of choice until granulated white sugar became affordable in the late 19th century.

Molasses is the syrup that arises during the cane sugar refining process. Sugar cane is crushed to pull out its juices, and the juice is heated to separate the sugar into crystals and syrup.

The process of refining sugar requires several stages. Molasses may come from the first stage, in which case it's called, fittingly enough, *first molasses*. (Later boilings of the molasses draw out more sugars and lead to darker and darker molasses.)

The darker the molasses, the less sweetness it's going to have. Molasses lends deeper and more complex flavors than table sugar; it's a little heartier and has a sharp tinge on the tongue that sugar doesn't give you.

Molasses doesn't just make pumpkin pie and gingerbread cookies taste good; it has a long history of use as a laxative, and currently blackstrap molasses (the darkest and most bitter form) has a reputation as a health boost, in part because of its high concentrations of iron and calcium. It also has an almost mythical status, drawing claims that it has cured cancer and arthritis and even restored natural color to gray hair. The jury's out on those bits, but a host of pit masters can attest to its benefits to barbecue sauce.

Sour notions

If you're going to have a little sweet in your sauce, you need some sour, too, to keep the mix from becoming more of a dessert glaze than a suitable topper for meat. Here are the most-used options:

- Lemon or lime juice
- Prepared mustard
- Vinegar
- Worcestershire sauce

Seasonings

Pungent fresh vegetables like onions, garlic, and peppers add a lot of depth (and in some cases a little sweetness) to your sauce. Dried herbs and spices go even farther. Less usually is more when it comes to seasonings, so proceed carefully as you season your sauce.

Here are some of the seasonings that commonly make it into barbecue sauces:

- Allspice
- Celery seed
- Cinnamon
- Garlic powder
- Ginger
- Onion powder

Chapter 5 runs down a lot of the surefire seasoning combinations.

Hot touches

Not every sauce is a hot sauce, but even sweet sauces do well with a little something spicy, which, if you add it with a very cautious hand, actually underscores the sweet effect you're going for.

Then, of course, there are four-alarm-fire sauces that throw the balance in the opposite direction, using a little something sweet to create depth and complement the tongue-scorching elements within the sauce.

Adding prepared hot sauce is a reasonable shortcut and creates good results. Here are some further suggestions for fueling a fire:

- Black pepper (fresh ground)
- Cayenne pepper
- Chili powder
- Chipotle (smoked jalapeño) peppers or sauce
- Cloves
- Crushed red pepper
- Dry mustard
- Horseradish
- Minced fresh hot peppers (jalapeño, habanero, serrano, and so on)
- Paprika
- Pure chile powders from ancho, pasilla, caribe, or other hot peppers

Smoke in a bottle

Given the provenance of barbecue and of smoking, it's ironic and just plain weird that you can now buy smoke in a bottle.

Liquid smoke is made from the condensed smoke coming off popular barbecue woods like hickory and mesquite as they're heated. The liquid is collected, filtered, and then bottled and shipped to the shelves of a grocery store near you. (Look for it among the condiments.)

In most cases, nothing goes into the bottle but the condensed smoke. Still, there's a distinct flavor about most liquid smoke products on the market that make it easily discernable from the flavor that slow-smoking provides. It's a shortcut, and short-cuts tend not to come off as well as the real thing.

Still, if you're time crunched or live in an apartment or anywhere else that keeps you from doing actual smoking (or if you just have no interest in the smoking process), liquid smoke is a viable alternative. Its flavor is super-concentrated, so you need only a few drops to give smoke flavor to a sauce. It's a nice touch for barbecue sauces, of course, and it may make more of your marinade, too. Liquid smoke also makes a showing in many cooks' salsas, and it jazzes up plain old ketchup for your hamburgers, too.

Finding Exotic Inspirations for Terrific Sauces

Traditional sauces are just that. They use ingredients that most people associate with barbecue (although in an endless variety of proportions and combinations). If you want to step outside the barbecue comfort zone, you might try working with some of the idea starters you find in Table 8-1.

Table 8-1 Inspirations for Unexpected Barbecue Sauces

Sauce	Ingredients
Hoisin	Soy sauce, black bean paste, white vinegar, sesame oil, brown sugar, garlic powder, hot sauce
Mole	Tomatoes, onion, chilies, garlic, peanuts, cinnamon, black pepper, salt, unsweetened chocolate, olive oil, chicken stock, sesame seeds
Peanut	Peanut butter, lime juice, cilantro, crushed red pepper, ginger

Sauce	Ingredients
Sweet and sour	Rice vinegar, ketchup, brown sugar, soy sauce, cornstarch
Tamarind chutney	Dried tamarind, dates, cumin, cayenne pepper, sugar, salt
Teriyaki	Soy sauce, ginger, Japanese rice wine, cider vinegar, sugar
Thai sweet chile	Serrano chili, ground red chile paste, rice vinegar, plum sauce, sugar, lime juice, tomato paste, garlic, paprika, salt
Tikka Masala	Tomato paste, heavy cream, vegetable oil, onion, garlic, ginger, fenugreek, cilantro, hot green chile pepper

Using plum sauce

Plum sauce is one element of the Thai sweet chile sauce in Table 8-1, and a good condiment all on its own. The tart and sweet sauce ends up on tables in most Chinese restaurants, and it can do good things for barbecue sauce, too.

Made with vinegar and sugar (and usually a few seasonings; ginger is a popular one), plum sauce has many of the elements you'd put into your sauce anyway, making it a fair shortcut. Plum wine makes a nice addition, too.

You can find plum sauce and plum wine (and other faces of Chinese plums, like dried or pickled versions that may also make interesting elements of sauce) in any Asian market.

Chapter 9

Crafting Barbecue Sauces Traditional and Unusual

● ●

In This Chapter

▶ Touring the sauce regions

▶ Mixing sauces of various styles

▶ Finding that perfect balance of sweet and heat

● ●

*B*arbecue sauce can cement friendships or end them. Feelings about
what makes a great sauce run deep, and
there's no sense trying to convince anyone
of your own preferences.

In this chapter, no side is taken, but the
wealth of recipes gives you plenty of room
to decide for yourself.

Tom Schneider kicks off the chapter with a
slew of recipes that give you the flavor of
the major barbecue regions of the United
States. And then he jumps out of the way
to give the floor to his esteemed fellow
competition cooks.

Touring American Barbecue Regions

Engineer by weekday, barbecue caterer
and competition barbecue cook by weekend, Tom Schneider has been an avid stu-
dent of barbecue since he first tried out a smoker more than a
decade ago.

In this section, Tom leads a tour of the American barbecue regional sauce styles. As you see from the recipes in this section, not everyone agrees about what makes good barbecue sauce.

In the competitive world of barbecue, one man's sauce is another man's punch line. For anyone whose sense of curiosity overpowers her competitive spirit, the range of sauces add up to a grand journey, and this section is a wild first leg.

Beale Street Memphis Sauce

Mustard, tomato, and vinegar are common characteristics of Tennessee sauces. Schneider says his Beale Street Memphis sauce is ideal for pulled pork, Memphis-style — drizzled on top of coleslaw piled atop the pork in a sandwich.

Preparation time: *5 minutes*

Cooking time: *20 minutes*

Yield: *About 3 cups*

2 cups ketchup	*1 teaspoon garlic powder*
½ cup cider vinegar	*1 teaspoon onion powder*
8-ounce can tomato puree	*1 teaspoon lemon juice*
¼ cup prepared yellow mustard	*1 teaspoon ground black pepper*
¾ cup brown sugar	*½ teaspoon salt*
2 tablespoons Worcestershire sauce	*½ teaspoon cayenne chili powder*

1 In a medium saucepan, combine all ingredients and stir well.

2 Place saucepan over medium-high heat and bring to a simmer. Reduce heat to low.

3 Simmer for 15 minutes. Remove from heat; cool.

Tip: *Make sure that the pan is cool when you add the mustard. The mustard distributes most effectively when it's cool.*

Originally, Memphis barbecue meant dry-rubbed ribs without sauce of any kind, and you still find many of the Memphis pit masters making their ribs that way. Sauce eventually trickled into the Memphis barbecue profile, and maybe because the area is closer to the Carolinas than it is to Kansas City, the sauce typically served there is heavy on vinegar and mustard — the hallmarks of Carolina sauces. When you do find sauce served with barbecue in Memphis, it's more likely to be on the side than it is to be drenched over the meat.

Texas sauces run the gamut; you're as likely to fine a sweet, thick sauce in Texas as you are to find a vinegary and spicy version. One thing you can count on is finding brisket (c'mon — this is cattle country) and hot links, spicy smoked sausages that are a product of German influence in the state.

Texas Steer Ranch Sauce

Schneider points out that Texas sauces can range from thick, tomato-based versions to the more commonly found thinner, peppery, and coffee-accented sauce with Tex-Mex-influenced seasonings. This one more closely follows the latter lines.

Preparation time: *5 minutes*

Cooking time: *15 minutes*

Yield: *About 3½ cups*

2 tablespoons butter	*1 tablespoon molasses*
2 cups ketchup	*1 teaspoon Tabasco sauce*
8-ounce can tomato puree	*1 teaspoon garlic powder*
¾ cup brown sugar	*1 teaspoon paprika*
½ cup cider vinegar	*1 teaspoon onion powder*
½ cup black coffee	*1 teaspoon salt*
2 tablespoons lemon juice	*1 teaspoon ground black pepper*
1 tablespoon chili powder	*¼ teaspoon cayenne chili powder*

1 In a medium saucepan, melt the butter over low heat.

2 Add the remaining ingredients. Stir well. Increase heat to medium and bring to a simmer.

3 Simmer for 15 minutes. Remove from heat; cool.

Note: *Instant coffee will work just fine for this recipe; add a teaspoon or two extra coffee crystals so the flavor will come through in the sauce.*

Hyping coffee for cooking

Given its traditional place as a with-dessert beverage, finding coffee in recipes for cakes and other sweets is no surprise. It's less common in savory recipes, but the same things that make it interesting in desserts make it a natural for sauces and dry rubs.

Within each puny bean you find a range of intense flavors — tastes that range from earthy to chocolaty and spicy to buttery. That complexity means that coffee complements pretty much anything and can bring out unexpected flavors in whatever you're cooking.

You find coffee in Tom Schneider's Texas Steer Ranch Sauce in this section.

Alabama White Sauce

Schneider notes that this sauce isn't one you're going to run into unless you're within the Alabama state lines, but it's a phenomenon in that area, popularized by one of the big names of Alabama barbecue — Big Bob Gibson Bar-B-Q, a longstanding restaurant.

Preparation time: *5 minutes*

Cooking time: *None*

Yield: *About 2 cups*

1½ cups mayonnaise	*1 tablespoon ground black pepper*
½ cup white vinegar	*1 teaspoon prepared horseradish*
2 tablespoons lemon juice	*1 teaspoon salt*
2 tablespoons white sugar	

    Whisk all ingredients together until smooth.

Note: *Baste chicken and ribs in the final minutes of grilling and serve as a dipping sauce. Store this sauce in the fridge for a night or so, and the horseradish flavor becomes more apparent.*

White sauce is a wild card of barbecue sauces. It somehow has earned legendary status without significantly venturing out of its home area.

You need to use care when you cook with it, because mayonnaise doesn't handle heat well. Your best bet is to baste it on during the last few minutes of cooking and serve more of it on the side. If you put on the white sauce too early, the mayonnaise separates and the sauce becomes less effective and much less appealing.

White sauce makes a good condiment for many different foods. You find another mayo recipe — for Anthony Hanslits's Wasabi Mayo — in Chapter 11.

Kansas City BBQ Sauce

The sweet, thick tomato sauces of the region have taken hold far outside Kansas city. "Kansas City is considered by some as the heart of the U.S. barbecue world," Schneider says, "but don't tell that to a Texan or a Carolinian."

Preparation time: *5 minutes*

Cooking time: *20 minutes*

Yield: *About 3 cups*

2 tablespoons butter	1 teaspoon garlic powder
2 cups tomato puree	1 teaspoon onion powder
¾ cup brown sugar	½ teaspoon ground celery seed
½ cup light corn syrup	½ teaspoon salt
½ cup vinegar	½ teaspoon ground black pepper
1 tablespoon chili powder	½ teaspoon cinnamon
1 teaspoon liquid smoke	

1 In a medium saucepan, melt the butter.

2 Add the remaining ingredients, gently stir, and then simmer for 15 minutes. Remove from heat; cool.

Kansas City–style barbecue sauce is kind of like reality TV: It has completely permeated American culture, and not for any good reason. Nothing about it makes it better for barbecue than, say, a vinegar or mustard sauce — even a mayonnaise sauce. In the democracy of sales figures, though, Kansas City barbecue sauce is elected by a landslide.

You find further versions of this thick, tomatoey, sweet sauce in the upcoming section, "Cooking Up More Classic Barbecue Sauces."

Carolina "East" Raleigh Sauce

This style of sauce meets the original standards for barbecue sauce — to simply tenderize and flavor the meat. Schneider's version sticks with Eastern Carolina traditions.

Preparation time: *5 minutes*

Cooking time: *15 minutes*

Yield: *About 1 cup*

1 cup cider vinegar	½ teaspoon ground black pepper
1 teaspoon red pepper flakes	1 tablespoon dark brown sugar (optional)
1½ teaspoons salt	

1 In a small saucepan, combine all ingredients and mix.

2 Simmer over low heat for 10 minutes. Remove from heat; cool.

Note: *Use this sauce as a baste over pork during smoking and as a dipping sauce.*

Carolina "West" Piedmont Sauce

This type of sauce starts off the same as its cousin out east, Schneider says, but may bring ketchup and molasses into the mix.

Preparation time: *5 minutes*

Cooking time: *20 minutes*

Yield: *About 1½ cups*

1 cup cider vinegar	½ teaspoon ground black pepper
½ cup ketchup	½ teaspoon dry ground mustard
½ teaspoon cayenne pepper	1 tablespoon dark brown sugar
1½ teaspoon salt	1 tablespoon Worcestershire sauce

1 In a medium saucepan, combine all ingredients and mix.

2 Simmer over low heat for 10 to 15 minutes. Remove from heat; cool.

Cooking Up More Classic Barbecue Sauces

Given the prevalence of thick, tomato-based sauces on grocery shelves and in barbecue joints around the country, it's no surprise that the recipes in this section contain several versions that fit in that category.

Little tweaks may have a ripple effect in a sauce, pulling out flavors you never knew were there, so within the tomato-based category lies a great deal of room for variation. And you're always welcome to modify at will. Think bourbon belongs in every sauce? I wouldn't argue. Like it heavy on mustard? Fire at will.

Original BBQ Sauce

You can't beat a classic. Or so says John Webb of the Up-in-Smoke team, who confesses that no matter how much he experiments, he always comes back to this basic sauce, which he uses with the Up in Smoke mop sauce you find in Chapter 10.

Preparation time: *5 minutes*

Cooking time: *15 to 30 minutes*

Yield: *About 2 cups*

2 teaspoons chili powder	1 tablespoon dried onions
4 heaping tablespoons dark brown sugar	1 cup apple cider
1 tablespoon salt	⅔ cup apple cider vinegar
1 tablespoon red pepper flakes	½ cup ketchup
1 tablespoon molasses	½ small red onion, chopped fine

1 In a medium saucepan, combine all ingredients and bring to a slow boil over medium heat.

2 Continue boiling 15 minutes, or until sauce thickens. Remove from heat; cool.

Note: *The sauce thickens further when you store it overnight in the fridge.*

Variation: *Sauté 3 minced garlic cloves in 1 tablespoon butter until caramelized. Add ½ cup red wine and simmer to reduce the wine to a couple tablespoons. Follow instructions for original sauce, reducing vinegar by ⅓ cup.*

Chipotle-Maple Barbeque Sauce

Maple syrup and minced chipotle peppers give Paul Kirk's recipe a smoky-sweet punch.

Preparation time: *10 minutes*

Cooking time: *30 minutes*

Yield: *About 2½ cups*

1 tablespoon canola oil

1 cup minced onion

2 large garlic cloves, pressed

1 cup canned chicken broth

1 cup ketchup

¼ cup real maple syrup

1 tablespoon minced chipotle pepper (canned in adobo sauce)

1 teaspoon sea salt

½ teaspoon fresh ground black pepper

½ teaspoon allspice

1 In a large saucepan, heat the oil and sauté the onion over medium heat for 5 minutes.

2 Stir in garlic and sauté 2 minutes.

3 Add remaining ingredients and bring to a boil.

4 Reduce heat and simmer 15 minutes, or until thickened.

5 Remove from heat and let cool.

6 Optional: Pour into food processor or blender and puree until smooth.

Chipotle peppers are a natural fit for barbecue because they have a similar provenance. Because jalepeño peppers rot quickly, they were smoked as a preservation method. The result is called a chipotle pepper.

You can buy whole chipotle peppers; a chipotle powder also is available. (It shows up in some of the recipes in this book.) The kind of chipotle you want for Paul Kirk's Chipotle-Maple Barbeque Sauce is the kind you find in cans with adobo sauce. These chipotles have been stewed in adobo, a sauce made from tomatoes, garlic, vinegar, a bunch of other chiles, and cinnamon, among other seasonings.

Chipotle peppers in adobo will keep in your refrigerator for a good long time (at least three months), but if you get antsy to use up what you have left over, you can easily puree the peppers with the adobo sauce and butter or mayo to create a nice topper for fish, especially shrimp.

If you're intense like that, you also can smoke jalapeños yourself to make your own chipotles. Instructions are at www.recipe source.com.

Rib Runner Sauce

The Rib Runners team uses this sauce on chicken and pork. They say plenty of trial and error brought them to the recipe.

Preparation time: *10 minutes*

Cooking time: *25 minutes*

Yield: *About 3½ cups*

¼ cup minced onion

2 cloves garlic, minced

1 tablespoon margarine

2 teaspoons chili powder

1 teaspoon ground black pepper

½ teaspoon cinnamon

1 cup chili sauce

½ cup Kraft honey barbecue sauce

½ cup Kraft original barbecue sauce

1 cup beef broth

2 tablespoons fresh lemon juice

1 tablespoon dark brown sugar

2 teaspoons Worcestershire sauce

¼ teaspoon liquid smoke

A few dashes red hot sauce

1 In a heavy stock pot, sauté the onion and garlic in margarine over medium heat.

2 Stir in the remaining ingredients.

3 Simmer 20 minutes. Remove from heat; cool.

Pork Sauce

As the name indicates, this sauce is a winner on pork, and the Pirates of the Grill team particularly advises that you use it for pulled pork.

Preparation time: *10 minutes*

Cooking time: *15 minutes*

Yield: *About 2½ cups*

1 cup ketchup	*1 tablespoon chili powder*
1 cup water	*1 teaspoon black pepper*
⅓ cup cider vinegar	*1 teaspoon molasses*
⅓ cup packed brown sugar	*½ teaspoon celery seed*
1 tablespoon onion powder	*½ teaspoon salt or seasoned salt*

1 In a medium saucepan, combine all ingredients and bring to a slow boil.

2 Reduce heat to medium-low and simmer until thickened, about 15 minutes. Remove from heat; cool.

Kentucky Bourbon BBQ Sauce

Tom Schneider says the bourbon and butter in his sauce give it a smooth, unique flavor, while the Worcestershire sauce (always part of the "Owensboro black" sauces in Kentucky) leaves a decided tang.

Preparation time: *10 minutes*

Cooking time: *20 minutes*

Yield: *About 3 cups*

2 tablespoons butter	*1 teaspoon garlic powder*
2 cups ketchup	*1 teaspoon onion powder*
1 cup brown sugar	*1 teaspoon lemon juice*
½ cup cider vinegar	*1 teaspoon ground black pepper*
¼ cup bourbon	*½ teaspoon chili powder*
¼ cup Worcestershire sauce	*½ teaspoon allspice*

1 In a medium saucepan, melt the butter.

2 Add the remaining ingredients.

3 Stir well, and then bring to a light simmer. Simmer for 15 minutes. Remove from heat; cool.

In northwestern Kentucky, the black sauce that originated in Owensboro sits on restaurant tables in bottles and is poured over meat, especially mutton (which has a strong flavor about it to begin with, coming as it does from older sheep, and can use a douse of strong flavor).

Big R's BBQ Sauce

Rick Soliman is the "Big R" of this sauce and the leader of the Smoke Hunters' team. He uses this sauce on chicken, pork, and beef.

Preparation time: 5 minutes

Cooking time: 15 minutes

Yield: About 1½ cups

1 cup ketchup	1½ teaspoons kosher salt
3 tablespoons apple cider vinegar	½ teaspoon hot sauce
2 tablespoons lemon juice	1 tablespoon garlic, minced
¼ cup brown sugar	½ cup water
2 teaspoons Dijon mustard	2 teaspoons Worcestershire sauce

1 In a medium saucepan, combine all ingredients and bring just to a boil.

2 Reduce heat and simmer for 10 to 15 minutes. Remove from heat; cool.

Bootheel BBQ Sauce

The Shigs-in-Pit team provides this recipe for a thinner, vinegar-style sauce that they recommend serving over hickory-smoked ribs.

Preparation time: 5 minutes

Cooking time: About 5 minutes

Yield: About 1½ cups

(continued)

(continued)

1 cup white vinegar

½ cup ketchup

1 tablespoon kosher salt

½ cup granulated sugar

2 teaspoons granulated garlic

1 tablespoon Worcestershire sauce

1 In a medium saucepan, combine all ingredients.

2 Over medium heat, whisk until completely dissolved and combined.

3 When mixture comes to a boil, remove pan from heat; cool.

Paradise BBQ Sauce

Brown sugar and molasses give the Pig Smokers in Paradise team's sauce an overt sweetness; jerk rub and chili powder keep it interesting.

Preparation time: *20 minutes*

Cooking time: *30 minutes*

Yield: *3½ cups*

½ green bell pepper, diced

½ red bell pepper, diced

½ medium white onion, diced

1 tablespoon oil

2 cloves garlic, minced

1 cup brown sugar

1 teaspoon molasses

¼ cup Worcestershire sauce

¼ cup prepared yellow mustard

2 teaspoons chili powder

2 teaspoons black pepper

1 teaspoon ground cumin

2 teaspoons Caribbean jerk rub

½ teaspoon garlic powder

½ teaspoon lemon juice

1 teaspoon kosher salt

1 tablespoon Tabasco sauce

3 cups ketchup

1 In a large saucepan or pot, sauté the bell pepper and onion in the oil for about 5 to 7 minutes.

2 Add the garlic and sauté 2 minutes more.

3 Add all the remaining ingredients except the ketchup, and allow the spices to dissolve.

4 Add the ketchup and simmer 30 to 45 minutes, stirring frequently. Remove from heat; cool.

5 Optional: For a smoother sauce, pour mixture into food processor or blender and puree until smooth.

The jazz on jerk

The jerk seasoning you need for the Paradise BBQ Sauce is easy enough to find on the shelves of any grocery store; the story behind the style of cooking that relies on it has a lot in common with barbecue. Jerk cooking is the Jamaican version of slow smoking, often done over a pit or a halved steel drum and using pimento wood. Rubs and marinades are a big part of the process, and the flavors that most commonly show up in jerk cooking include Scotch Bonnet chilies, allspice, cinnamon, ginger, and thyme. Like *barbecue,* the origin of the term *jerk* is up for debate, with some theories attributing it to a Spanish word for dried meat or from the practice of jerking cooked meat from a pig carcass.

Maple Syrup Barbeque Sauce

Maple syrup and brown sugar provide the sweetness in this well-balanced sauce from Paul Kirk.

Preparation time: *10 minutes*

Cooking time: *20 minutes*

Yield: *About 3 cups*

1 cup pure maple syrup	2 tablespoons olive oil
1 cup ketchup	2 tablespoons Worcestershire sauce
1 cup minced onion	2 teaspoons chopped garlic
¼ cup brown sugar, packed	1 teaspoon salt
¼ cup cider vinegar	¼ teaspoon hot sauce
¼ cup fresh lemon juice	2 teaspoons lemon zest
¼ cup water	

1 In a large saucepan, combine all ingredients and bring to a boil.

2 Reduce heat and simmer 20 minutes. Remove from heat; cool.

3 Pour into food processor or blender and puree until smooth.

Spiced Mustard Sauce

When you're ready for something other than the common red barbecue sauce, give this mustard version from Rich Allen of Dick's Bodacious Bar-B-Q, Inc., a whirl.

Preparation time: *5 minutes*

Cooking time: *10 minutes*

Yield: *About 1 cup*

½ cup Dijon mustard

½ cup apple juice

½ cup packed brown sugar

1 tablespoon crushed red pepper

1 teaspoon garlic powder

1 teaspoon coarse ground black pepper

1 In a small saucepan, combine all ingredients.

2 Simmer over medium heat for 10 minutes, stirring frequently with a whisk. Use immediately or store in the refrigerator in an airtight container.

Bringing Fruit Flavor to Sauces with Juices and Jams

Fruit offers a fuller-bodied kind of sweetness than does white sugar, which has nothing but sucrose in its flavor profile. The extra depth makes using fruit juices and jellies a fantastic way to sweeten your sauces.

Honey-Orange BBQ Sauce

Roger Mogg of the Smoky River BBQ Team cooked by feel until his wife explained the error of his ways. This recipe, which he says he uses just like ketchup, is the first one he committed to paper.

Preparation time: *5 minutes*

Cooking time: *30 minutes*

Yield: *About 2 cups*

1½ cups ketchup

½ cup apple cider vinegar

½ cup brown sugar

6 tablespoons honey

2 tablespoons orange juice

2 tablespoons pineapple juice

1 tablespoon Worcestershire sauce

½ tablespoon liquid smoke

½ tablespoon onion powder

½ tablespoon garlic powder

½ tablespoon black pepper

1 tablespoon chili powder

¼ teaspoon ginger

½ teaspoon red pepper

½ teaspoon paprika

1 In a medium saucepan, combine all ingredients and bring to a boil.

2 Bring sauce to boil.

3 Reduce heat and simmer 30 minutes, stirring occasionally, or until sauce thickens. Remove from heat; cool.

Variation: *Try grapefruit or other citrus juices in place of the orange or pineapple juice. Add a teaspoon or two of cayenne or habanero powder to spice things up.*

Apple Barbecue Sauce

Paul Kirk gives his apple barbecue sauce a unique, savory edge with fresh minced ginger.

Preparation time: *5 minutes*

Cooking time: *20 minutes*

Yield: *About 1½ cups*

½ cup apple jelly

8-ounce can tomato sauce

¼ cup sweet rice wine vinegar

2 tablespoons light brown sugar

2 tablespoons apple juice

1 teaspoon grated fresh ginger

1 teaspoon Louisiana hot sauce

½ teaspoon sea salt

1 In a medium saucepan, combine all ingredients and mix.

2 Bring to a boil, stirring until smooth.

3 Reduce heat, and simmer about 10 to 15 minutes, stirring occasionally. Remove from heat; cool.

(continued)

(continued)

   Tip: Freeze ginger root before you use it. Frozen ginger is easier to handle and slice or grate than warmer ginger. And you can store the root in your freezer for a few months without harming it.

Louisiana hot sauce is any thin, bottled hot sauce that's made from red chiles and vinegar. Several hot pepper sauces, Tabasco included, fit into this category. The Original Louisiana Hot Sauce is a milder version of the form.

You can find hot sauces that reach into high end of the Scoville scale that measures capsaicin to indicate the "heat" of a pepper. The hottest pepper on record measures up to 1 million Scoville units, but some sauces claim to reach more than 10 million Scoville units. (You find out more about measuring the heat of peppers in Chapter 11.)

Harvest Apricot Sauce

Ginger and jalapeño bite through the sweetness of the apricots, giving this sauce a perfect balance of sweet and hot. Rich Allen, founder of Dick's Bodacious Bar-B-Q, Inc., created this recipe.

Preparation time: *5 minutes*

Cooking time: *10 minutes*

Yield: *About 1 1/2 cups sauce*

10-ounce can apricot preserves	*1 teaspoon garlic powder*
½ cup apple cider vinegar	*1 teaspoon onion powder*
¼ cup soy sauce	*1 fresh jalapeño, seeded and minced*
1 tablespoon prepared mustard	*1 teaspoon coarse ground black pepper*
1 teaspoon ground ginger	

1 In a small saucepan, combine all ingredients.

2 Simmer over medium heat for 10 minutes, stirring frequently with a whisk. Use immediately or store in the refrigerator in an airtight container.

Chapter 10

Getting Saucy while You Cook: Mop Sauces

A lesson learned the hard way by almost every beginning cook is that barbecue sauce can't stand the heat. Traditional barbecue sauce burns, as does most heavy sauce with a tomato or sugary base. Brush it onto chicken or ribs early in the cooking, and you end up with a blackened exterior instead of the full, toothsome flavor (and texture) you were looking for.

Enter mop sauces. These lighter sauces are formulated not only to add flavor and juiciness to your meat but to do it on a hot grill or in a smoker.

You use mop sauces to add moisture to meat and, if they include an acid like vinegar or citrus juice, to help keep it tender. You can make them from just a few ingredients or using other barbecue elements you may have on hand, which means that mop sauces are an easy area to dip your toes into the waters of experimentation.

Here are a few suggestions for crafting a mop without too much trouble:

> ✔ **Make use of marinade.** Boil any leftover marinade to make sure it's free from bacteria, and then dilute it with water. You can use vinegar or a light fruit juice to dilute it, but only if those ingredients show up in the marinade. Using something with a strong flavor will throw off the balance of your intended flavors, so proceed carefully.

✔ **Start with your dry rub.** Combine a few tablespoons of your dry rub with about a pint of apple juice or cider vinegar — or both.

✔ **Thin your barbecue sauce.** If you use a low-sugar barbecue sauce, you can dilute it with water, juice, or vinegar until it's the right watery consistency for mopping.

✔ **Bring beer to the task.** Add beer to your rub or barbecue sauce to create a mop. Beer is slightly acidic, and it adds moisture and a gentle, usually pretty neutral flavor that isn't going to stomp all over the other flavors in your cooking. And, you know — it's practically a staple, so you're likely to have some on hand.

If you really want to keep things simple, just bust out the apple juice. Pour some in a spray bottle and spritz it onto the meat while it cooks. Apple juice adds moisture, and it's mild enough that it won't assert itself over the primary flavors from the meat or your seasoning rubs. Apple juice also adds a touch of color and sheen to ribs or chicken.

No matter which mop sauce you decide to use, you want to brush or spray it onto the meat you're cooking approximately every half-hour.

In this chapter, you find easy recipes for the sauces that can take the heat.

Finding further uses for hardworking beer

Even if drinking it were the only good purpose beer had going for it, the stuff would never go out of fashion. Turns out beer is like an all-purpose fix-it, bake-it, clean-it, and more for household jobs. Kind of like vinegar, only much better for drinking.

Here are several more projects you can assign to beer:

✔ **Washing your hair:** Boil it first to take out the drying alcohol, and then wash your hair with beer. Makes it extra shiny.

✔ **Keeping your copper clean:** Beer's mild acidity makes it a swell way to put a shine on copper.

✔ **Saving your vegetation:** Slugs love beer but don't know how to stop. Bury a few jars half-filled with beer in the yard before bed, and you wake up to a whole mess of drunk, drowned slugs in the morning. Beer also is rumored to improve brown spots in your lawn.

Making Mops Especially for Pork

Pork dries out easily, but mopping it regularly while it cooks staves off the unappealing desiccation.

Because of fears of the once-common (and extremely uncomfortable) parasitic infection trichinosis, pork often is overcooked by wary grillers and smokers. The reality is that trichinosis now is very rare, in large part because of improved feeding and handling practices.

Bourbon Que Mop Sauce for Pork Tenderloin

Bourbon shows up in a goodly number of sauce recipes, and why not? It not only provides acidity and rich earthiness but also gives a cook something to sip while he works. This recipe from Paul Kirk uses butter to beef up the richness factor and add further acidity.

Preparation time: *5 minutes*

Cooking time: *5 minutes*

Yield: *About ¾ cup*

1 whole lemon	1 tablespoon grated onion
½ cup soy sauce	¼ teaspoon hot sauce
3 tablespoons butter	⅛ teaspoon sea salt
2 tablespoons bourbon	⅛ teaspoon fresh ground black pepper

1 Cut the lemon in half and squeeze the juice into a small saucepan.

2 Throw the lemon halves into the pan.

3 Turn heat to medium-high and add remaining ingredients, stirring to combine.

4 Reduce heat and simmer 5 minutes.

Note: *Brush over tenderloin before cooking, and mop sauce onto meat regularly as it cooks.*

Mopping Sauce for Pork Ribs

Charlie Lamb of Charlie's Butcher Block swears by this deceptively simple, super-tasty mop recipe.

Preparation time: *5 minutes*

Cooking time: *None*

Yield: *2½ cups*

1 cup vegetable oil
1 cup apple cider vinegar

½ cup Worcestershire sauce

In a medium bowl, combine all ingredients.

Smoke Hunters BBQ Mop

Try The Smoke Hunters' mop recipe on ribs or pork shoulder. (For the team's sauce recipe, Big R's BBQ Sauce, turn to Chapter 9.)

Preparation time: *5 minutes*

Cooking time: *10 minutes*

Yield: *About 2¼ cups*

2 cups apple or pineapple juice
1 stick butter

½ cup brown sugar.

In a medium saucepan, combine all ingredients and stir over medium heat until sugar has dissolved.

Butch's Whole Pig Basting Sauce

Butch Lupinetti did, in fact, throw down Bobby Flay on the cooking competition show "Throwdown! with Bobby Flay," where he outcooked the snarky chef in a barbecue competition. His basting sauce brings a lot of heat to whatever you use it on.

Preparation time: *5 minutes*

Cooking time: *About 10 minutes*

Yield: *About 2 gallons*

1 gallon apple cider vinegar

4 cups cayenne pepper

1 gallon water

1 cup brown sugar (or to taste)

6 lemons sliced in ¼-inch slices

1 chopped onion

2 tablespoons chopped garlic

2 to 3 tablespoons Butch's Smack Your Lips Magic Dust (or your own seasoning rub)

In a large pot, bring all ingredients to a boil. Inject or mop pig generously. Can also be used as a sopping sauce to dip your cooked meat into — as long as you like it hot.

Biting into a whole-hog cooking project

Butch's basting sauce recipe makes enough for a whole hog, but you don't have to use it that way. If you're thinking about smoking a whole hog, keep in mind that for every 25 pounds of dressed pig, you get about 10 pounds of meat. And buying a whole hog isn't like picking up a chicken on the way home from the office — make sure you give your butcher at least a week's notice.

Also, you need a grate that's about 4 feet wide to accommodate a whole hog. Unless they own monster smokers, most people dig pits and line them with stones or build temporary pits from concrete blocks and a metal screen. Don't forget about the charcoal, either: For a 100-pound hog, you need a good 60 pounds of the stuff.

Finally, unless you're using a rotisserie, butterflying the hog is the best way to get it to cook evenly. To butterfly the hog, you need to split the rib bones from the spine without breaking the skin along.

Concocting Multipurpose Mops

An acid and a lot of liquid are the critical points of a mop sauce; where you take it from there can be very different depending on the seasonings you throw into the mix.

The following recipes highlight particularly versatile mop sauces.

Spicy Mop Sauce

The red pepper flakes in this recipe from Grillmaster's Garden give a subtle heat to this mop sauce. Let the sauce sit in the fridge for an hour or two to give the heat a chance to permeate the liquid and give a better balance to the sauce.

Preparation time: *5 minutes*

Cooking time: *None*

Yield: *About 2 cups*

1 teaspoon black pepper	3 tablespoons sugar
1¼ cups cider vinegar	½ teaspoon kosher salt
⅔ cup water	1 teaspoon red pepper flakes

In a medium bowl, combine all ingredients.

Variation: *You can also use this sauce as a marinade. It works well with any meat. Just soak it in the marinade in the refrigerator according to the time suggestions you find in Chapter 4.*

The multipurpose mop

You're more likely to use a basting brush or small mop brush to apply them to whatever you're cooking, but mop sauces may have gotten their name from early cooks' using cotton rag mops (the very kind you may use to clean the kitchen floor) to baste large amounts of meat while it smoked. They'd dip the thing in basting liquid and heft it up over the meat to coat a lot of it in one sweep. When you consider that a lot of mop sauces include vinegar — as famous for its cleaning power as for its meat-tenderizing properties — maybe the practice really wasn't much of a stretch.

Up in Smoke Mop Sauce

John Webb from the Up-in-Smoke team uses this mop sauce along with his Original BBQ Sauce (see Chapter 9).

Preparation time: *5 minutes*

Cooking time: *None (but need to let sit overnight)*

Yield: *2 cups*

1 cup vinegar	1 tablespoon dark brown sugar
1 cup apple cider	1 tablespoon red pepper flakes
1 tablespoon salt	1 tablespoon fresh ground black pepper

1 In a storage container, combine all ingredients and shake.

2 Let sauce sit in the refrigerator overnight to let flavors combine.

Chapter 11

Sauces and Relishes for Dipping and Dashing

Man cannot live by barbecue sauce alone. Or maybe he could, but variety does a body good, and in this chapter you find some of the also-rans — sauces that don't quite qualify for the label *barbecue sauce*, at least not traditionally speaking. Maybe they're a little off the beaten path or maybe they don't even come near the path, but each, in its own special way, does something great for the meat that you barbecue or grill.

This chapter gives you good ideas for topping fish and even hamburgers, for serving alongside chicken, pork, steak, and pretty much anything else you may smoke or grill.

In the pages ahead, you find a recipe for a helluva hot sauce as well as one for a rich dipping sauce. There's a full section full of sweet sauces and a fantastic formula for bourbon-onion chutney.

Fanning the Flames with a Hotter-Than-Hot Sauce

Chiles have been cultivated and have been an important part of cooking for thousands of years. Given their legendary status — hot peppers have been attributed with a number of health benefits including increasing the metabolism, fighting back cancer, and even eradiating vertigo — chiles show no signs of letting up their hold on the imagination and palate.

The havoc chiles wreak on your tongue is nothing compared to what they'll do to other tender tissues. Your best bet is to wear rubber gloves when you handle particularly hot peppers. Barring that, make sure you wash your hands thoroughly after you're done touching the peppers. Rubbing your eyes with a hand still doused in *capsaicin* — the compound that provides chiles' heat — is an agony that doesn't soon dissipate.

Porkrastinators Pepper Medley Hot Sauce

Take a look at the first three ingredients, and you can see why Team Porkrastinators issues a warning with this recipe: Use it sparingly, they say, because it packs a mother of a wallop.

Preparation time: *5 minutes*

Cooking time: *30 minutes*

Yield: *About 1½ cups*

3 jalapeño peppers	*1 cup water*
4 habanero peppers	*1 cup cider vinegar*
3 cayenne peppers	*1 teaspoon salt*
6 cloves garlic	*1 teaspoon brown sugar*
1 carrot	*½ teaspoon cumin*
½ medium onion, chopped	

1 In a medium saucepan, combine all ingredients and bring to a boil.

2 Reduce heat to low.

3 Let mixture simmer until peppers have softened, about 30 minutes.

4 Pour mixture into blender and puree until smooth.

Tip: *Because this recipe produces such a scorcher of a hot sauce, you may want to tone it down. Just cut out the habanero peppers (the hottest chilies the recipe includes) or, if you want to keep that particular flavor, use only one, and reduce the number of cayenne and jalapeños that you use by one.*

The hottest hot pepper?

Scoville units measure the amount of capsaicin in a pepper. A standard orange habanero pepper has a reputation as a real killer and measures somewhere around 100,000 to 350,000 Scoville units. (The wide variation is a product of the differences in growing conditions.)

The red savina pepper is a cultivar of the habanero and one that took over its top spot on the Scoville scale. It has a rating of 350,000 to 580,000 units.

But in 2005, the red savina lost its throne by a long shot when the Bhut Jolokia was shown to measure 1 million Scoville units. Grown under controlled conditions and tested at New Mexico State University's Chile Pepper Institute, the pepper unseated the red savina in the Guiness World Records in 2007.

Your impulse when something too hot hits your tongue may be to slug back water, but doing so only moves the pain-inducing chemicals around in your mouth, causing further discomfort. Milk or yogurt coats your mouth and braces it for the abuse you're giving it. Taking a bite of something bland like rice or bread also can cut back the afterburn.

Part of the reason hot peppers are so hard to stop eating is because of the pain they inflict. The injury capsaicin causes your tongue also leads to the release of endorphins, the body's natural painkillers; basically, the pain leads to a feel-good effect. Less scientifically, most people experience a misguided inclination to take one more bite to ease the pain. And when that doesn't work? Another.

Sweetening the Pot: Sauces with a Softer Side

Failing to explore the spectrum of food flavor is selling your tongue short — and it may even mess with your health.

Many nutritionists and dietary experts recommend that you include something to target each of the five primary taste sensations (sweet, sour, bitter, salty, savory) in a meal to best feel sated when you're finished. The theory goes that when you offer a bit of each to your tongue, your brain calls it a meal much sooner than it would had you stuck with just one type of taste.

The recipes in this section give you tasty ways to test the theory by working some sweetness into your meals.

Blueberry Balsamic Barbeque Sauce

Brandon Hamilton dreamed up this recipe as a way to use up all those extra blueberries you tend to have at the end of the blueberry season. It's a light and summery recipe that partners well with duck, chicken, seafood, and even beef.

Preparation time: *10 minutes*

Cooking time: *30 minutes*

Yield: *1½ cups*

2 cups fresh (or frozen) blueberries	3 tablespoons ketchup
½ cup balsamic vinegar	2 tablespoons lemon juice
¼ cup apple juice	2 garlic cloves, chopped
3 tablespoons lemon juice	1 teaspoon cardamom
3 tablespoons honey	1 pinch salt

1 In a saucepan, combine all ingredients.

2 Bring mixture to a boil; then reduce heat and simmer 30 minutes or until sauce starts to thicken, stirring occasionally.

3 Remove pan from heat, and cool.

4 Transfer sauce to a blender, and process until smooth. Place in a plastic container with a lid and refrigerate up to 5 days.

Cardamom shows up in a lot of Indian recipes, because the plant that it comes from is native to the area. What you buy in a jar is either whole or ground seeds from the pod of the plant (although you also can buy whole pods), and the plant itself is part of the same family from which ginger and turmeric hail.

Cardamom has a sharp, almost orangey flavor that makes it a great match for many fruits. A sprinkle in ground coffee also does interesting and tasty things for your morning cup.

Bourbon Onion Chutney

A *chutney* is a condiment made from fruit and vegetables. Chutneys turn up a lot in Indian cooking. Brandon Hamilton developed this chutney with bourbon so that it goes especially well with grilled steak or pork chops.

Preparation time: *15 minutes*

Cooking time: *About 40 minutes*

Yield: *About 2 cups*

2 tablespoons vegetable oil	*2 tablespoons molasses*
2½ cups chopped yellow onion	*⅛ teaspoon ground allspice*
1 teaspoon mustard seeds	*½ cup water*
½ cup bourbon	*2½ ounces chopped dried apricots*

1 In a heavy 12-inch skillet, combine the oil, onions, and mustard seeds, and cook on medium heat until the onions begin to turn golden brown, about 15 minutes.

2 Deglaze the pan with the bourbon, and then add molasses, allspice, water, and apricots.

3 Bring the chutney to a simmer and cook until thick, about 15 minutes. When the mixture is thick, remove from heat, place into a plastic container, and refrigerate.

Tip: *Adding liquid to a pan after you've roasted meat (or, in this case, caramelized onions) gives you a way to pick up the flavorful browned bits from the pan and incorporate them into a sauce. Deglazing describes the process, but all it really means is that you add liquid where you really didn't have any. Doing so ensures that you make use of all the flavor instead of leaving behind what otherwise might cling to the pan.*

Bourbon and barbecue have a long history together, maybe because both issue from the southern United States, maybe because bourbon, like smoked meat, takes on flavors from wood.

Bourbon isn't bourbon unless it's been aged for two years in a white oak barrel.

Apricot Preserve Dipping Sauce

Ginger is a great complement to the apricot preserves in this recipe from Anthony Hanslits.

Preparation time: *15 minutes*

Cooking time: *40 minutes*

Yield: *About 1½ cups*

10-ounce jar apricot preserves	1 inch ginger, unpeeled and thinly sliced (about 18 slices)
⅓ cup soy sauce	
2 tablespoons ketchup	3 teaspoons lemon juice

1 In a saucepan, combine apricot preserves, soy sauce, ketchup, and ginger. Bring to a boil over medium heat.

2 Reduce heat and simmer 30 minutes.

3 Strain liquid into a plastic container. Stir in lemon juice. Label, date, and initial.

Honey BBQ Wing Sauce

Use Paul Kirk's recipe as a finishing sauce by brushing it onto any cut of cooked chicken, or as a wing sauce by tossing it in a large bowl with cooked wings.

Preparation time: *5 minutes*

Cooking time: *20 minutes*

Yield: *About 2 cups*

1¼ cups ketchup	1 teaspoon liquid smoke
⅓ cup white vinegar	½ teaspoon salt
¼ cup molasses	¼ teaspoon onion powder
¼ cup honey	¼ teaspoon chili powder

1 In a small saucepan, combine all ingredients.

2 Bring to a boil over medium heat, stirring often.

3 Reduce heat and simmer 15 to 20 minutes. Use immediately or store in an airtight container in the refrigerator.

Taking an Exotic Turn with Sauces That Cull Asian Flavors

Barbecue as we know it today has been around for about two centuries, max. Cooks in Asia have been at it for thousands of years. Safe to say, we could learn a thing or two from them, and in this section, you find recipes that borrow flavors and methods from the much-older cuisine.

Indian Tamarind Sauce

Used in India as a condiment for a range of dishes, this sauce, interpreted here by Brandon Hamilton, has balanced flavors of tart and sweet that pair well with spicy or sweet barbecue. The tartness of the tamarind goes well with chicken, fish, and beef.

Preparation time: *10 minutes*

Cooking time: *20 minutes*

Yield: *About 1 cup*

2 tablespoons all-purpose flour

1¼ cup cold water

6 tablespoons tamarind concentrate (available at most Asian markets)

1 teaspoon ground mustard seeds

1 teaspoon ground cumin

½ teaspoon cayenne

½ teaspoon cardamom

½ teaspoon salt

1 tablespoon sugar

1 Place the flour in a small bowl and stir in 2 tablespoons of the cold water to make a smooth paste. Set aside.

2 In a small saucepot, combine remaining ingredients.

3 Place saucepot over medium heat and bring sauce to a simmer. Lower heat and continue to cook for 10 minutes.

4 Mix 2 tablespoons of the sauce into the flour mixture and stir until flour mixture is combine with sauce.

5 Now mix the flour mixture into the sauce in the saucepot. Stir until well combined.

6 Continue to cook until the sauce stars to thicken, about 5 minutes.

Tip: *If you want, you can strain the sauce before you use it to remove the seeds.*

Chinese Hoisin Barbecue Sauce

Brandon Hamilton developed this sauce to incorporate the Chinese hoisin sauce into a wonderful barbecue sauce that works well with chicken, seafood, pork, vegetables, and beef.

Preparation time: *5 minutes*

Cooking time: *None*

Yield: *About 1 cup*

½ cup hoisin sauce	2 tablespoons grated fresh ginger
¼ cup honey	1 tablespoon minced garlic
2 tablespoons sherry	3 green onions, finely chopped
2 tablespoons fresh lime juice	1 teaspoon ground black pepper
2 tablespoons soy sauce	1 teaspoon sesame oil

1 In a mixing bowl, combine all ingredients except for the oil and mix together gently with a whisk.

2 When the ingredients are thoroughly mixed, add the oil and mix until combined. This recipe stays good for 5 days in the refrigerator.

You should be able to find hoisin sauce in your supermarket, but if you're having trouble, try an Asian market, which will offer up several choices.

The thick rust- or brown-colored sauce is made from soybeans, garlic, vinegar, as well as seasonings and sweeteners that vary from sauce to sauce. It's a little bit sweet and has a flavor all its own — a little salty, very strong, often spicy.

In China, hoisin is used on its own as a dipping sauce or as an ingredient in other sauces.

Wasabi Mayo

Anthony Hanslits' wasabi mayo recipe is a tasty topper for grilled or smoked salmon and a great dip for fries. Try it on hamburgers, or even use it to make a spicy slaw.

Preparation time: *5 minutes*

Cooking time: *None*

Yield: *About 2 cups*

1 cup wasabi powder	½ tablespoon salt
½ cup water	1 cup mayonnaise
1½ tablespoons lemon juice	

1 In a mixing bowl, place the wasabi powder. Add the water and mix until it forms a smooth paste.

2 Add the lemon juice and salt, and mix.

3 Add the mayonnaise, and stir until all ingredients are combined.

4 Place in a new plastic container. Label, date, and initial.

Peanut Dipping Sauce

A winner with a range of meats or with grilled vegetables, this peanut dipping sauce from Grillmaster's Garden works particularly well with chicken.

Preparation time: *10 minutes*

Cooking time: *About 10 minutes*

Yield: *About 1½ cups*

½ cup chunky peanut butter	¼ teaspoon chile oil
¼ cup lime juice	¼ cup chopped fresh cilantro
⅓ cup soy sauce	¼ cup sliced green onions
¼ cup sesame oil	½ cup water
3 tablespoons sugar	1 teaspoon cornstarch
1 teaspoon red pepper flakes	

1 In a saucepan, combine peanut butter, lime juice, soy sauce, sesame oil, sugar, red pepper flakes, chile oil, cilantro, and onions.

2 Bring to a simmer over medium-low heat.

3 In a small bowl, mix water and cornstarch until well blended.

4 Add the water-cornstarch mixture to the saucepan and stir until the sauce has thickened slightly.

5 Remove from heat and let cool in the refrigerator before serving.

 Peanut butter becomes especially fragrant when you heat it. You may want to open some windows or make the sauce a day before you plan to invite people over so the heavy aroma has a chance to dissipate.

Cool Summery Takes on Sauces, Salsas, and Relishes

Fruits and vegetables are a clear partner for outdoor cooking, given that both become more common in the summer. Chicken sided with a ginger cucumber relish or grilled fish topped with fresh fruit salsa make for memorable meals.

This section provides smart ways for using the bright flavors of summer.

Guacamole Sauce

A great side for chicken or an excellent dip for snacking, this guacamole sauce from Grillmaster's Garden is mild and refreshing.

Preparation time: *5 minutes*

Cooking time: *None*

Yield: *About 2½ cups*

3 ripe avocados, pitted and scooped from the skins (see instructions following this recipe)

Juice of 1 lemon

½ teaspoon cayenne pepper

¾ cup plain yogurt

1 teaspoon salt

2 tomatoes, seeded and chopped

2 green onions, sliced thin

1 In a blender or food processor, combine the avocado, lemon juice, pepper, yogurt, and salt.

2 Process until sauce becomes smooth.

3 Transfer to a bowl, and stir in the tomatoes and green onions.

Pitting an avocado is easier the riper the avocado, and you may be able simply to scoop out the pit with a spoon. If not, use a chef's knife to twist out the pit. Follow these steps (and Figure 11-1):

1. **Cut the avocado in half lengthwise.**

2. **Hold the half with the pit in your hand, peel-side down.**

3. **Swing the knife into the pit, using the weight of it and its momentum to bury it down into the pit a third of the way or so.**

4. **Twist out the pit.**

5. **Use a spoon to scoop out the fruit.**

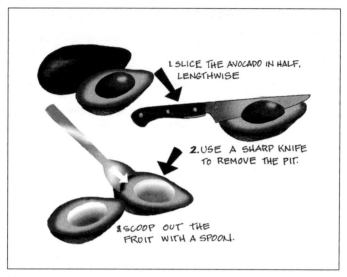

1. SLICE THE AVOCADO IN HALF, LENGTHWISE

2. USE A SHARP KNIFE TO REMOVE THE PIT.

3. SCOOP OUT THE FRUIT WITH A SPOON.

Figure 11-1: Pitting an avocado.

Ginger Tomato Relish

Brandon Hamilton's relish recipe takes advantage of the bounty of tomatoes that summer brings. The flavors are very crisp and clean and go well with grilled meats, chicken, or fish. The relish also works all on its own as a salad.

Preparation time: *20 minutes*

Cooking time: *None, but 30 minutes to chill*

Yield: *About 5 cups*

¼ cup apple rice vinegar

2 teaspoons sugar

3 teaspoons peeled and minced ginger

⅓ cup peanut oil

1 medium green bell pepper, chopped

4 green onions, finely chopped

4 cups halved pear tomatoes

1 In a medium bowl, whisk together the vinegar, sugar, and ginger.

2 Gradually whisk in the oil.

3 Mix in the onions and green bell pepper.

4 Add the tomatoes to the relish base and toss to combine.

5 Season with salt and pepper to taste.

6 Place in a plastic container and refrigerate 30 minutes.

Ginger Cucumber Relish

Relishes are served as an accompaniment for many different meat items in a whole range of cultures. This one from Brandon Hamilton matches up with grilled chicken, roasted duck, and grilled fish.

Preparation time: *10 minutes*

Cooking time: *None, but estimate 1 hour to allow flavors to mingle and the cucumbers to soften*

Yield: *About 3½ cups relish*

2 English cucumbers, peeled, halved, seeded, cut crosswise into ¼-inch-thick slices

2 teaspoons salt

½ cup rice vinegar

⅓ cup brown sugar

2 tablespoons minced peeled ginger

1 teaspoon ground cumin

⅛ teaspoon cayenne pepper

1 In a mixing bowl, combine cucumbers with salt and gently toss.

2 In a separate bowl, combine the vinegar, sugar, ginger, cumin, and cayenne pepper mix until the sugar is dissolved.

3 Mix the vinegar solution into the cucumbers and toss until combined.

4 Place into a plastic container and cover. Let the relish set for 1 hour.

 English cucumbers are pretty close to seedless, so you can use them as they come. If you substitute a standard slicing cucumber (which in addition to seeds, has a thicker skin), you may want to cut the cucumber in half lengthwise and scrape out the seeds with a spoon. There's no harm in eating the skins, but from a texture standpoint, scraping off some of the peel doesn't hurt.

Chilean Fruit Salsa

Grillmaster's Garden offers this vibrant salsa and recommends serving it atop grilled salmon.

Preparation time: *5 minutes plus 1 hour for chilling*

Cooking time: *None*

Yield: *About 3 cups*

1 cup plums, diced (about 3 plums)	½ red onion, chopped
1 cup kiwi, diced (2 kiwis)	½ jalapeño, chopped
2 tablespoons chopped fresh cilantro	Juice of 1 lime
½ ripe avocado, diced	Salt and pepper, to taste

1 In a medium bowl, combine all ingredients and mix.

2 Cover and let sit in refrigerator about 1 hour, to allow flavors to blend.

Part IV

Entrees and Sides and Then Some

The 5th Wave   By Rich Tennant

"I'm not sure what flavor you're tasting. I didn't use any spice rubs on the meat. However, I dropped it several times on the way to the pit."

In this part . . .

Dr. Atkins aside, most people like a little something nestled up against their barbecued ribs or smoked chicken — a spoonful of baked macaroni and cheese, maybe, some coleslaw, or even stuffed dates if you're throwing tradition to the wind (and why wouldn't you?). In this part, I give you a treasury of recipes for dishes handed down through generations and modern concoctions.

Chapter 12

Something(s) to Serve with Your Barbecue

*B*aked beans and macaroni and cheese have been making it onto barbecue plates practically since the dawn of smoking, but how about parmesan-stuffed dates, pizza bread with crispy prosciutto, or stuffed jalapeño peppers?

In this chapter, you find dishes traditional and unusual, many of which you cook right on your grill or smoker.

Beans, Beans: The Most Magical Food

Cook them in your smoker, on your grill, on the stove, or in the oven, and baked beans tend to please crowds. They're a cookout staple and a wildly adaptable one, at that.

The recipes in this section provide three very different takes on the long-loved classic, starting with a version closest to traditional and moving through versions spicy and smoky.

Loophole's Baked Beans

Baked beans have been nuzzling up next to brisket and ribs and such since the beginning of barbecue. Stink-Eye BBQ provides this version, which improves on the sweetish classic by including spicy sausage.

Preparation time: *20 minutes*

Cooking time: *45 minutes*

Yield: *10 servings*

¼ pound lean ground beef

¼ pound spicy sausage

2 15-ounce cans pinto or white beans

2 cups ketchup

1 cup mustard

2 cups brown sugar

½ large onion, diced

¼ cup Worcestershire sauce

1½ tablespoons cinnamon

1 tablespoon vanilla

½ teaspoon cayenne pepper

2 cloves garlic, minced

¾ cup barbecue sauce

1 Brown ground beef and sausage.

2 Drain the meat.

3 In large bowl, mix beans, ketchup, mustard, brown sugar, onion, Worcestershire, cinnamon, vanilla, cayenne, garlic, and barbecue sauce.

4 Stir in beef and sausage.

5 Pour into 3-quart casserole pan.

6 Bake at 350 degrees for about 45 minutes.

Smoky Black Beans

The smoked pepper powder and chipotle chilies give Paul Kirk's black bean dish a smoky overtone.

Preparation time: *20 minutes*

Cooking time: *20 minutes*

Yield: *12 servings*

1 small onion, minced

2 teaspoons olive oil

1 or 2 chipotle chilies (canned in adobo sauce), minced

4 15-ounce cans black beans, drained and rinsed

¾ cup fresh orange juice

2 fresh tomatoes, skinned (see the "Skinning tomatoes" sidebar), deseeded, and chopped

1 teaspoon chipotle powder or smoked habanero powder

Salt and pepper, to taste

1 In a 2-quart heavy stockpot, cook the onion in the oil over low heat, stirring until onion has softened.

2 Add chilies and continue cooking, stirring regularly, for 2 minutes.

3 Add beans, water to cover, and orange juice.

4 Mash lightly with a potato masher.

5 Add tomatoes and chipotle powder and simmer mixture for 15 minutes.

6 Season with salt and pepper.

Tip: *If tomatoes are out of season or if you just want to make things a little easier on yourself, substitute a 15-ounce can of diced tomatoes for the fresh version. Throw in the whole can with all the tomato juices.*

Santa Fe Pinto Beans

Paul Kirk's take on beans tweaks the typical sweet baked variety with a touch of chilies.

Preparation time: *15 minutes*

Cooking time: *25 minutes*

Yield: *10 servings*

1 medium green bell pepper, diced	15-ounce can black beans, drained
1 medium onion, chopped	15-ounce can pinto beans, drained
2 garlic cloves, minced	10-ounce can diced tomatoes with green chilies, undrained
1 tablespoon olive or canola oil	
14½-ounce can chicken broth	10-ounce package frozen corn, thawed
½ teaspoon cumin	1 tablespoon red wine vinegar

1 In 2-quart heavy stockpot, sauté green bell pepper, onion, and garlic in oil for 3 minutes.

2 Stir in chicken broth and cumin.

3 Bring mixture to boil.

4 Reduce heat, cover, and simmer for 15 minutes.

5 Add beans, tomatoes, corn, and vinegar, and heat through, simmering another 15 minutes.

Skinning tomatoes

Tomato skins can add a bitter flavor to recipes, which is why some call for the skins to be removed — a feat that takes a little getting used to. To skin a tomato, follow these steps:

1. **Wash the tomato and remove its stem.**

2. **Scratch an *X* on the bottom of the tomato to give yourself a place to start peeling when the time comes.**

3. **Fill a medium mixing bowl halfway with ice and water. Set aside.**

4. **Bring a pot of water to a boil.**

5. **Drop the tomato into the boiling water.**

6. **Remove it with a slotted spoon as soon as you see the skin start to peel.**

7. Place the tomato immediately Into the ice bath.

8. Let the tomato cool in the ice bath for at least 5 minutes.

9. Pull the skin from the tomato, using a paring knife to nudge away any stubborn bits from the tomato.

Baking Unique Sides in the Smoker or on the Grill

Impress your friends and amaze your neighbors by baking biscuits or making pizza outside in your smoker or on your grill. (Of course, you also can make these recipes in the oven, if you'd rather, but it's not nearly as cool.)

Iron Skillet Potato Bacon Biscuits

Cook up Paul Kirk's savory biscuits in your grill or smoker.

Preparation time: *15 minutes*

Cooking time: *About 15 minutes*

Yield: *6 servings (2 each)*

⅓ cup butter

1 cup self-rising soft-wheat flour

1 cup potato flakes

½ cup shredded cheddar cheese

8 slices bacon, cooked crisp and crumbled

¾ cup buttermilk

¼ cup melted butter

1 Grease a 9-inch iron skillet or baking pan with shortening.

2 Cut ⅓ cup butter into flour and potato flakes with a pastry knife until mixture is crumbly.

3 Add cheese, bacon, and buttermilk.

4 Stir until dry ingredients are moistened.

5 Turn dough onto floured surface and lightly knead three or four times.

6 Roll or pat dough to ¾-inch thickness.

7 Using 2½-inch round cutter, cut out 12 biscuits and place in skillet.

8 Bake in smoker or grill (using indirect heat — see Chapter 2) at 425 degrees 12 to 14 minutes.

9 Brush tops with melted butter.

Tip: *Baking these biscuits in an 425-degree oven works well, too.*

Pizza Bread with Roasted Cherry Tomatoes and Crispy Prosciutto

Salty, crispy prosciutto gives this recipe, from Grillmaster's Garden, a lot of snap, but in a pinch, you can substitute plain old bacon.

Preparation time: *30 minutes*

Cooking time: *30 minutes*

Yield: *6 to 8 servings*

Dough:

½ cup hot water (115 to 120 degrees)

1 package active dry yeast

½ teaspoon sugar

½ teaspoon salt

½ teaspoon oil

½ tablespoon dried oregano

1½ cups all-purpose flour

Toppings:

14 ounces cherry tomatoes

1 tablespoon olive oil

Salt and pepper, to taste

4 ounces prosciutto, chopped and fried crispy

4-6 ounces fresh mozzarella

4 tablespoons fresh basil, chiffonade (see Tip at end of recipe)

1 In a large bowl, mix the water, yeast, sugar, 1 teaspoon salt, ½ teaspoon oil, and oregano.

2 Let mixture stand 5 minutes.

3 Gradually add flour until dough pulls away from bowl.

4 Knead dough by hand for 5 minutes.

5 Brush a clean, large mixing bowl with olive oil.

6 Place kneaded dough into greased bowl and let rise 1 hour or until dough has doubled in size.

7 While dough rises, preheat grill to 425 degrees.

8 Toss tomatoes with oil, salt, and pepper and place on baking sheet.

9 Bake on grill for 15 to 30 minutes, or until tomatoes have softened. Set aside.

10 Remove dough from bowl and knead for 5 minutes.

_11_ Roll out dough to desired thickness (about ⅛ inch), dusting with flour as necessary to keep dough from sticking. Transfer dough to an oiled piece of foil.

_12_ Allow dough to rise for a few minutes.

_13_ Using a fork, poke several holes in pizza dough.

_14_ Top with 1 tablespoon olive oil, roasted tomatoes, prosciutto, and mozzarella.

_15_ Grill directly on grate at about 425 to 450 degrees for 4 to 7 minutes.

_16_ Remove from grill and top with fresh basil.

Tip: _Chiffonade means "cut into shreds." The easiest way to cut these very thin strips of basil is to stack the leaves, roll them end to end, and slice strips from the roll._

Preparing Potatoes with a Plethora of Approaches

Bless the versatile spud, so adaptable to growing conditions and kitchen conditions, so ready to be mashed, baked, or fried. It's a particularly gregarious vegetable, playing nicely with about anything you throw at it.

This section gives you recipes that blend potatoes with barbecue techniques and flavors.

Super Spud Casserole

This decidedly rich and exceptionally simple potato casserole recipe comes from Paul Kirk.

Preparation time: _10 minutes_

Cooking time: _1 hour_

Yield: _6 to 8 servings_

½ cup sharp grated cheddar cheese	_1 bell pepper, chopped_
½ cup grated mozzarella cheese	_2 cups chopped ham or pulled pork_
2 cans cream of potato soup	_1 cup diced bacon_
2-pound bag frozen hash browns	_8 ounces sour cream_

1 Combine cheeses and reserve ¼ cup of mixture.

2 In a large bowl, mix soup, hash browns, bell pepper, ham or pork, bacon, and sour cream.

3 Pour mixture into one 13-x-9-inch or larger glass dish.

4 Sprinkle remaining ¼ cup of cheeses over top of casserole.

5 Bake on grill or in smoker or oven for 1 hour at 350 degrees.

In the United States, you most commonly see only a few varieties of potatoes. In South and Central America (where potatoes originate), cooks have dozens upon dozens of potato types to work with.

Potatoes have something in common with barbecue: They came into prominence as a staple of the underprivileged. Potato plants are extremely easy to grow and not terribly fussy about where you plant them. They're kind of like the tuber equivalent of pigs, which eat anything and can handle most climates.

Mississippi Potatoes

This is a goes-with-just-about-anything and easy-to-make casserole from Paul Kirk.

Preparation time: *10 minutes*

Cooking time: *1 hour*

Yield: *8 to 10 servings*

8 cups cooked and diced potatoes	*½ cup chopped onion*
1 cup mayonnaise	*4 to 6 slices bacon, cooked crisp and crumbled*
1 teaspoon salt	
½ teaspoon pepper	*½ cup green olives*
1 pound processed American cheese, diced	

1 In a large mixing bowl, toss potatoes with mayonnaise, salt, pepper, cheese, and onion.

2 Place mixture in greased 10-x-14 baking dish.

3 Sprinkle with bacon and olives.

4 Bake at 325 degrees for 1 hour.

Shamrock Golden Tubers

The Smokin' Irish BBQ Team points out that, in the motherland, potatoes are called "tubers," and they round out a barbecue on either side of the pond. You can whip up these tubers on the smoker, on the grill, or in the oven.

Preparation time: *20 minutes*

Cooking time: *1 to 2 minutes*

Yield: *8 to 10 servings*

Special equipment: *Mandoline*

8 ounces Irish cheddar cheese (Kerrigans or Dubliner), shredded

3 pounds Yukon gold potatoes

1 stick butter, divided into 16 pieces

3 cloves garlic, minced

1 medium onion, sliced thin

Salt and pepper, to taste

1 Reserve ½ cup of the shredded cheese.

2 Spray a 3-quart casserole dish with cooking spray.

3 Using a mandoline, slice potatoes to about⅛-inch thick.

4 Add one layer of potatoes to casserole dish.

5 Top with about one quarter of the garlic, onions, and cheese.

6 Add salt and pepper.

7 Repeat layers until you've used up all the potatoes, garlic, onions, and butter (four pats of butter per layer), adding salt and pepper to each layer.

8 Layer remaining cheese over the top.

9 Cover with lid or aluminum foil and cook on smoker or grill for about 1½ to 2 hours at 250 degrees, or in a 375-degree oven for about 45 minutes.

A *mandoline* is a hand-operated slicer that works magic by slicing vegetables in any of several configurations. You can use it to get uniform slices — thick or thin — or to julienne (cut into strips like French fries) vegetables or even to dice onions.

You can find mandolines in a lot of variations (and in prices from $20 to $120 or so) — made from wood, plastic, or stainless steel and with varying degrees of adjustment — but they're all long and narrow, with a main blade and several attachment plates that you use according to the kind of cuts you want to get. The suckers are sharp, so you use a guide that comes with the mandoline to hang onto vegetables while you slice them.

Making Yer Mama Proud: Recipes for Veggies

Nothing is outside the reach of the smoker or grill. Certainly not asparagus, jalapeños, or green bell peppers, as the recipes in this section show.

Smokey Joel's Grilled Asparagus with Garlic and Butter

Joel Schwabe, head cook of the Smokey Joel team in Chicago, says that this recipe is good with just about any vegetable and recommends trying it with ¼-inch slices of zucchini or ½-inch slices of portobello mushrooms.

Preparation time: *10 minutes*

Cooking time: *10 minutes*

Yield: *2 to 4 servings*

1 bunch asparagus (20 to 25 pieces)	3 tablespoons butter
1 tablespoon canola oil	1 clove minced garlic
Salt and pepper, to taste	

1 Preheat grill to medium heat.

2 Trim tough ends (last 1 to 2 inches) off asparagus.

3 Place oil on sheet of aluminum foil.

4 Roll asparagus in oil to coat.

5 Sprinkle with salt and pepper.

6 Place asparagus (on foil) on grill and cook 5 minutes.

7 Turn asparagus and grill 5 more minutes.

8 While asparagus cooks, place butter and garlic in saucepan atop grill.

9 Remove pan when butter is melted.

10 Place cooked asparagus on fresh plate, and pour butter sauce over it.

Swinetology Smoked Stuffed Jalapeño Peppers

The Church of Swinetology team warns that although these stuffed peppers are addictive, making them is a little "like a game of Russian roulette" at first. Until you get the hang of choosing jalapeños that meet the spice level you can handle, you may end up with a few that run past your comfort zone. What's life if not lived on the edge, anyway?

Preparation time: *20 minutes*

Cooking time: *60 to 90 minutes*

Yield: *6 to 8 servings*

12 large jalapeño peppers	8-ounce package mild or sharp shredded cheddar
1 package bread stuffing	
1 cup Andouille sausage, chopped fine	Barbecue sauce

1 While wearing rubber gloves, cut the stem ends off the peppers and deseed them with a paring knife.

2 Wash peppers inside out, and let them dry.

3 Prepare bread stuffing according to package instructions.

4 In a medium skillet, cook the sausage over medium heat.

5 Drain sausage and set aside.

6 Put half of the stuffing into a bowl with the cheese and sausage and mix thoroughly.

7 Push the stuffing mixture into peppers, and then top off each pepper with bread stuffing at the open end.

8 Place peppers upright in grill pan (see Tip following this recipe).

9 Smoke peppers at 225 degrees until peppers are hot and soft, approximately 1 to 1½ hours.

10 Serve with barbecue sauce.

Variation: *Use pulled pork, bacon, breakfast sausage (or any other type of sausage) in place of Andouille.*

TIP

To make a grill pan, start with an aluminum vegetable pan (which has holes on the bottom) or punch holes in an aluminum pan. Stretch two layers of aluminum foil over the top of the pan and crimp foil around the pan's edges. Poke pencil-size holes in the foil 2 inches apart and secure the peppers by forcing the bottom tips of the peppers through the holes in the foil. Figure 12-1 shows you how.

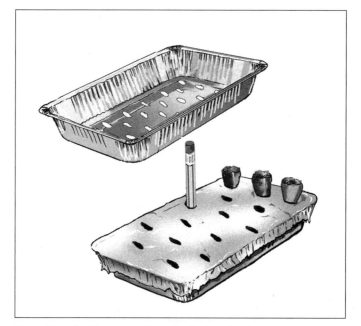

Figure 12-1: Fashioning a grill pan for Swinetology's peppers.

Roasting peppers

When you roast a pepper, you blacken the skin. Even better, you bring out the sugars and a unique, smoky flavor. It works best over a flame (simply hold it over the flame with tongs until the skin blackens), but you can do it in a broiler, too.

Here's how to roast a pepper:

1. **Rub olive oil over the pepper.**

2. **Hold it over a flame or put it under the broiler, turning until all sides are blackened.**

3. **Put peppers in a paper bag and fold over the top.**

4. **Allow peppers to steam for 20 minutes.**

5. **Remove peppers from bag and scrape off blackened skin.**

6. **Cut peppers open and remove stem, seeds, and membranes.**

Stuffed Peppers

Chef JJ of Grillmaster's Garden started making these peppers as a healthier alternative to fried jalapeño poppers but found that people tended to eat twice as many of them, so that kind of threw out the health benefits he was shooting for.

Preparation time: *About 20 minutes*

Cooking time: *1 hour*

Yield: *6 servings*

2 tablespoons olive oil

1 white onion, minced

2 garlic cloves, minced

2 jalapeños, roasted (see the "Roasting peppers" sidebar), seeded, and chopped

½ bell pepper, roasted (see the "Roasting peppers" sidebar), seeded, and chopped

½ cup fresh cilantro, minced

1 teaspoon hot sauce

1 teaspoon ground cumin

16-ounce can Bush's vegetarian baked beans, drained but not rinsed

12 ounces shredded pepper jack cheese

Salt and pepper, to taste

5 mild peppers, such as poblano or Anaheim

1 Preheat a grill set up for indirect cooking (see Chapter 2) to 400 degrees.

2 Preheat a cast iron skillet over medium-high heat.

3 Add olive oil, onions, garlic, jalapeños, and bell pepper.

4 Sauté mixture until onions have softened.

5 Lower heat and add cilantro, hot sauce, cumin, baked beans, and cheese.

6 Add salt and pepper.

7 Halve each of the five mild peppers and deseed them.

8 Brush lightly with olive oil and season with salt and pepper.

9 Fill each pepper half with bean mixture and set on a baking sheet.

10 Add wood chips to grill.

11 Grill peppers for 10 to 14 minutes, or until they've darkened and softened slightly.

Note: *If you prefer to make this recipe without leaving the house, use the stovetop for steps 1 through 6, and then cook the peppers in a 400-degree oven.*

Mixing Salads, Making Memphis-Style Slaw

Slaw is an important part of barbecue, and this section includes a recipe from one of the four barbecue regions. Pasta salad may not have quite as long a history, but it has made it into the lineup at pretty much every backyard party of the past several decades, so it clearly has earned its spot at the table. This section also includes a spinach salad recipe that has a long reputation as a crowd pleaser.

Warm Apple Spinach Salad

Dr. Chuckie's BBQ offers this award-winning recipe, which Dr. Chuckie himself says is the first thing to disappear at any potluck dinner that he brings it to.

Preparation time: *15 minutes*

Cooking time: *10 minutes*

Yield: *6 to 8 servings*

4 slices bacon	1 tablespoon Dijon mustard
1 small red onion, chopped fine	1 tablespoon salt
1 cup apple cider	2 10-ounce bags of spinach
2 tablespoons cider vinegar	

1 Cook the bacon slices and set aside.

2 Remove most of the bacon grease from the pan and then cook the onion over medium heat until it's barely tender, about 2 minutes.

3 Add the apple cider, cider vinegar, mustard, and salt.

4 Heat mixture through, but do not bring to boil.

5 Put the spinach in a large bowl.

6 Pour the warm vinaigrette over the spinach.

7 Crumble bacon over top.

Variation: *After adding vinaigrette, try mixing in water chestnuts, feta cheese, and/or raisins into the salad.*

Memphis Slaw for Pulled Pork

Coleslaw can be a traditional side dish for barbecue in many regions, with subtle variations in texture and twang. Tom Schneider, who runs Poppi-Q BBQ and who contributed to this book, prefers a crispy version, not soggy or finely chopped, with a little heat and sweet. He recommends trying it as part of a pulled-pork sandwich with a little barbecue sauce drizzled over the top.

Preparation time: *10 minutes*

Cooking time: *None*

Yield: *10 to 12 servings (about 9 cups)*

5 cups coarsely chopped green cabbage	*¼ cup brown sugar, packed*
3 cups coarsely chopped red cabbage	*1 tablespoon Dijon mustard*
½ cup shredded carrots	*1 tablespoon prepared horseradish*
1½ cups salad dressing (Miracle Whip or similar)	*1 teaspoon white pepper*
	¾ teaspoon celery seeds
¼ cup cider vinegar	*½ teaspoon salt*

1 In a large bowl, lightly toss the cabbage and carrots.

2 In a separate medium bowl, combine remaining ingredients and mix until well distributed and smooth.

3 Refrigerate at least 2 hours until chilled.

4 Just before serving, pour over cabbage and carrot mixture while tossing lightly. Serve as side or pulled pork sandwich topper.

Tom's recipe calls for prepared horseradish, which you find in jars in the condiment section of the grocery store. Horseradish starts as a root and is then grated and mixed with distilled vinegar and in many cases (depending on who's making it) oil, and some salt and a little sweetener.

Horseradish lends an intense and unmistakable flavor to whatever you put it in. (Bloody Mary, anyone?) It doesn't heat up until you hurt it. Break it open or have at it with a grater, and its defense system kicks in, releasing a strong irritant — the very thing that provides the root's heat when you use it in recipes. Distilled vinegar stabilizes the stuff, keeping it in top form for spicing up your salads, dips, and such.

Mount Vernon Macaroni Salad

An annual tradition for the Shigs in Pit team when it competes at the King City Showdown in Mount Vernon, Illinois, this recipe feeds the team members and their friends and family after the stress of the competition is over.

Preparation time: *10 minutes*

Cooking time: *None, but let sit at least 1 hour and preferably overnight*

Yield: *10 servings*

1 pound macaroni, cooked according to package instructions

1 carrot, grated

1 celery stalk, chopped

½ medium green bell pepper, chopped

1 cup sweetened condensed milk

2 cups Miracle Whip

1 cup sugar

½ cup white vinegar

1 teaspoon salt

¼ teaspoon black pepper

1 In a large bowl, combine the macaroni, carrot, celery, and green bell pepper.

2 In a separate mixing bowl, stir together the sweetened condensed milk, Miracle Whip, sugar, vinegar, salt, and pepper.

3 Add dressing to pasta mix.

4 Refrigerate about at least an hour and preferably overnight before serving.

To Macaroni and Cheese and Beyond

Rich, cheesy sides cozy up nicely to sharp, smoky barbecue flavors, and this section provides some creative ways to test that theory, as well as a real butt-kicker of a macaroni and cheese formula.

Parmesan-Stuffed Dates Wrapped with Bacon

Grillmaster Garden's stuffed dates make a unique hors d'oeuvre that's sweet and savory.

Preparation time: *15 minutes*

Cooking time: *15 minutes*

Yield: *8 servings (2 each)*

16 dates, pitted

8 slices bacon, cut in half

16 small pieces Parmesan or other hard cheese

1 Set up grill for indirect cooking (see Chapter 2) and preheat to 400 degrees.

2 Place a small piece of cheese into each date.

3 Wrap ½ slice bacon around each cheese-stuffed date.

4 Place prepared dates onto baking sheet.

5 Bake on grill for 12 to 15 minutes, or until bacon begins to crisp.

Variation: *Finish the dates over direct heat for a more rustic effect. You can also go in the other direction and bake the suckers in the oven.*

Dates don't have a long history with barbecue, given that they're grown primarily in the Middle East, but Paul Kirk is the Baron of Barbecue, and that counts for something. A fruit of the date palm, dates are eaten just as they are, dried, or made into vinegar, wine, paste, or syrup. The flowers of the date palm are edible, and even the leaves are cooked and eaten.

Blue Blazers

The rich, cheesy spread in this recipe from Paul Kirk gives a nice contrast to spicier dishes.

Preparation time: *10 minutes*

Cooking time: *10 minutes*

Yield: *8 servings*

¼ cup butter at room temperature

2 ounces Maytag blue cheese at room temperature

1 tablespoon cognac

¼ cup grated Parmesan cheese

¼ cup chopped, toasted walnuts

2 tablespoons minced green onion

1 teaspoon chopped fresh basil

Cayenne pepper, to taste

8 English muffins

Three olives (your choice), sliced

1 In a medium mixing bowl, mix the butter and blue cheese.

2 Stir in the cognac, Parmesan cheese, walnuts, onions, basil, and pepper.

3 Lightly toast the English muffin halves.

4 Spread the cheese mix on top of each muffin half.

5 Top each muffin half with an olive slice.

6 Brown lightly under the broiler (or in your smoker).

Cheesy Butternut Squash

This side-dish recipe won the Pepperitaville team first place in the Central Illinois Bragging Rights BBQ Contest in Arthur, Illinois.

Preparation time: *30 minutes*

Cooking time: *20 minutes*

Yield: *4 to 6 servings*

1 butternut squash	1 cup milk
2 eggs	1 cup freshly grated Parmesan cheese
¾ cup sour cream	2 cups shredded cheddar cheese
4 ounces cream cheese, at room temperature	1 tablespoon Creole seasoning

1 Preheat oven to 350 degrees.

2 Cut off both ends of squash, slice squash in half lengthwise, scoop out seeds and peel.

3 Cut the squash into ¾-inch cubes.

4 Put cubes in a glass baking dish, cover with plastic wrap, and microwave for 10 minutes.

5 While squash cooks, whisk eggs and sour cream.

6 Add cream cheese, milk, ⅔ cup of the Parmesan, 1½ cups of the cheddar, and Creole seasoning.

7 Uncover the dish and drain the squash.

8 Fold the squash into the cheese and egg mixture.

9 Spray a 9-x-9-inch baking dish with cooking spray.

10 Spoon the squash mixture into the baking dish.

11 Sprinkle the remaining Parmesan and cheddar cheeses over the top.

12 Bake approximately 30 minutes or until lightly browned and bubbly.

Variation: Use zucchini or any other squash in place of butternut.

Artisan Macaroni and Cheese

Executive Chef Michael J. Pivoney runs the Marion Street Cheese Market in Oak Park, Illinois, and fittingly offers a superb recipe for mac and cheese that runs rings around the standard version.

Preparation time: *10 minutes*

Cooking time: *20 minutes plus 20 minutes to bake*

Yield: *8 to 10 servings*

8 ounces aged cheddar (see note), finely shredded

4 ounces Gruyère cheese, finely shredded

1 pound premium-quality macaroni

1 tablespoon canola oil

1 tablespoon unsalted butter

2 cloves garlic, crushed fine

1 medium sweet onion, finely diced

1 tablespoon all-purpose flour

½ cup white wine

2 cups milk

1 cup heavy cream

4 ounces cream cheese

Pinch of cayenne pepper

Pinch of grated nutmeg (three gratings)

Salt, to taste

1 Preheat oven to 350 degrees.

2 Measure 1 tablespoon of the cheddar and 1 tablespoon of the Gruyère; set aside.

3 Cook macaroni according to package instructions, boiling only until al dente.

4 Meanwhile, in a medium saucepan, heat the oil and butter over medium heat until butter is melted.

5 Add garlic and onion, and sauté over medium-low heat for approximately 3 to 4 minutes, or until onion is translucent.

6 Add flour and stir constantly until well combined, approximately 4 minutes.

7 Pour wine into sauce and cook over medium heat an additional 3 to 4 minutes or until mixture is reduced by half.

8 Stir in milk and cream, and simmer about 5 minutes.

9 Over medium heat, gradually add the cheddar, Gruyère, and cream cheeses 1 tablespoon at a time, alternating the cheeses and stirring constantly, until the sauce becomes smooth.

10 Season with pepper, nutmeg, and salt.

11 Pour macaroni into greased 10-x-14 casserole dish.

12 Pour sauce over the top and sprinkle with the reserved cheddar and Gruyère cheeses.

13 Bake at 350 degrees until top browns, about 20 minutes.

Note: Pivoney recommends Widmer's Cheese Cellars or Hook's Cheese six-year aged versions of cheddar cheese.

Chili Dip

This no-fuss recipe comes from BBQ by Dan. You can find more of Dan's recipes at www.bbqbydan.com.

***Preparation time:** 5 minutes*

***Cooking time:** 10 minutes*

***Yield:** About 3½ cups dip*

12-ounce can of chili without beans

12-ounce can of chili with beans

¾ pound cube of Velveeta

8-ounce container of sour cream

4-ounce can of chopped green chilies

1 In saucepan, heat both cans of chili and Velveeta until the cheese has melted and is well blended with the chili.

2 Blend in sour cream and green chilies.

3 Serve warm with tortilla chips or the dip conveyance of your choosing.

Note: Dan says not to let this one get cold so it stays creamy and dippable. Keeping it warm in a slow cooker will help it last through the party.

Chapter 13

A Melange of Main Dishes

In This Chapter

▶ Using your grill or smoker in nontraditional ways

▶ Cooking great meals outside

▶ Finding different uses for barbecue cuts

*U*sing the techniques in Chapter 4 and the recipes in the earlier chapters, you can pull together no end of great meals. In this chapter, I give you some inspiration for putting everything together.

Here, I give space to some of the dozens of recipes that teams submitted for grilling. (Even devout barbecue worshippers bust out the grill on occasion, as you find in the pages to come.) You also find here a recipe for making a calzone in a smoker — who knew? — and for bringing a brisket to a tasty end right inside the house. Other recipes give you further opportunity to use your barbecue skills in ways traditional and not so.

Brisket: Out of the Smoker and into the Soup Pot

The very thing that makes brisket such excellent fodder for slow smoking is the thing that makes it a good choice for soups and stews, as well: its abundance of connective tissue.

Brisket comes from the chest area of the cow and includes the pectoralis muscle. Because it comes from such a hardworking area, the muscle is well developed and tough, a condition that lends itself not at all to the hot-and-fast methods of cooking like grilling.

Give a brisket a chance to break down all that connective tissue, though, and you're steps from paradise. Simmering it in liquid takes you there.

Vegetable Brisket Soup

No reason to reserve brisket for the smoker. Doug Golden of JD's Barbecue Shoppe browns it up and throws it into vegetable soup, which is a great way to take advantage of this tough cut.

Preparation time: *15 minutes*

Cooking time: *About 2 hours*

Yield: *4 to 6 servings*

1 pound beef brisket, cut into small pieces	1 cup sliced carrots
4 cups beef broth	½ cup corn
1 medium onion, chopped	1 cup sliced celery
3 cups water	1 cup green beans
1 14½-ounce can crushed tomatoes	½ cup frozen peas
1½ cups cubed potatoes	½ to 2 teaspoons herbs of your choice (basil, oregano, or dill)

1 In heavy stockpot, brown beef over medium-high heat.

2 Add onions and cook for 3 minutes.

3 Add water, beef broth, and tomatoes and simmer until beef is tender, about 90 minutes.

4 Add potatoes, carrots, corn, celery, and green beans, and cook until tender, about 30 minutes.

5 Add peas and herbs, and simmer another 2 minutes.

A Little Something Fabulous for Cooking Fish

Fish lends itself well to the hot-and-fast cooking you get from grilling, but with a caveat: Fish is much more delicate than pork, chicken, beef, or lamb and requires a little more care to keep it intact on the grill.

When you plan to cook fish on the grill, make sure you start with a nice, clean grill grate. You may also want to give the grate a light coating of oil before you cook your fish. Because most fish flakes, getting it stuck to the grill can sink your project.

Sea Bass with Nectarine Salsa

Jon Carr from Grillmaster's Garden uses a rich-tart marinade of coconut milk, lime juice, and curry powder to start off this recipe with a bang.

Preparation time: 15 minutes

Cooking time: 10 minutes

Yield: 4 servings

1 cup unsweetened coconut milk	2 cups cubed nectarines, in ¼-inch pieces
5 tablespoons fresh lime juice	
1 tablespoon curry powder	3 tablespoons diced poblano peppers
4 pieces Chilean sea bass, 6 to 8 ounces each	1 tablespoon diced fresh cilantro
	1 tablespoon diced fresh mint
Kosher salt, to taste	

1 In a mixing bowl, combine coconut milk, 1 tablespoon of the lime juice, and curry powder.

2 Season the sea bass with salt and place in the marinade, covering completely.

3 In a fresh mixing bowl, combine the nectarines, peppers, cilantro, and mint with the remaining 4 tablespoons of lime juice.

4 Grill the sea bass over medium-hot coals, about 4 minutes per side, or cook it in marinade in a 400-degree oven for 10 minutes.

5 Place cooked fish on plate and top with salsa.

Smoking Traditional Barbecue Cuts Like a Champ

They don't call it "Championship Chicken" for nothing, and in this section you get one team's formula for winning smoked chicken, as well as recipes for other standard barbecue cuts like ribs and pulled pork.

Chapter 4 gives you further details about the methods that these recipes cover.

Championship Chicken

Doug Spiller of Smoked Signals BBQ uses brine, a sweet rub, and an even sweeter spray to cook chicken that doesn't even need sauce.

Preparation time: *45 minutes*

Brining: *1 to 3 hours*

Cooking time: *About 2 hours*

Yield: *8 servings*

Brine

2 quarts water

2 quarts tangerine/grapefruit juice

1 cup sugar

¾ cup salt

4 pounds chicken, either bone-in pieces or a whole chicken

1 Combine ingredients in a Dutch oven or stockpot and heat, stirring, just until the salt and sugar dissolve, about 5 minutes. Cool completely.

2 Place chicken in brine.

3 Let stand 1 to 1½ hours for chicken parts, 2 to 3 hours for a whole bird.

Rub

½ cup granulated sugar

2 tablespoons brown sugar

¼ cup salt

¼ cup paprika

1 tablespoon dried celery leaves

1 tablespoon onion powder

1 tablespoon black pepper

½ tablespoon poultry seasoning

¼ tablespoon garlic powder

1 In small bowl, combine all ingredients.

2 Pat onto chicken over and under the skin. Let rest 30 minutes.

Super Chicken Spray

¼ *cup Triple Sec*   ¼ *cup apple juice*

Combine ingredients in spray bottle.

Chicken

1 Place chicken in a 280-degree smoker.

2 Let cook for 1 hour, being careful not to use too much wood, because chicken absorbs smoke quickly.

3 Raise temperature to about 350 degrees for 10 to 15 minutes to crisp the skin and bring chicken to finishing temperature (about 180 degrees internally).

4 Spray chicken after it's fully smoked.

Variation: *Grill chicken after spraying to crisp the skin.*

Putting triple sec to work in the kitchen

Triple sec is a liqueur that hails from France (where *sec* means *dry*) and traditionally is flavored with orange peels. It provides orange flavor without a lot of extra sweetness.

In case you're buying a bottle just for this recipe (and it's good enough that you shouldn't hesitate), here are further uses for the stuff:

✔ **Mixing cocktails, of course:** Use it in drinks like the margarita, cosmopolitan, Long Island iced tea, and Mexican sunset.

✔ **Flavoring fruit salad:** Just mix triple sec with an equal part orange juice and pour over any mix of fruit.

✔ **Adding snap to French toast:** Drop a couple tablespoons of triple sec into the batter.

✔ **Enlivening desserts:** Add a tablespoon of triple sec to a cup of whipped cream to add a crisp orange flavor and cut back the sweetness a smidge.

Jon's Baby Backs

Chef JJ of Grillmaster's Garden gives this rub a tinge of smokiness with a little chipotle pepper powder.

Preparation time: *20 minutes plus marinade time*

Cooking time: *4 hours*

Yield: *1 cup rub (about 8 servings for the ribs)*

½ cup brown sugar	1 tablespoon garlic powder
4 tablespoons granulated sugar	1 tablespoon kosher salt
4 tablespoons paprika	2 tablespoons onion powder
2 tablespoons chipotle powder	1 teaspoon cayenne pepper

1 Combine all ingredients in a large mixing bowl.

2 Stir or shake to mix. Use immediately or store in an airtight container.

Ribs

4 racks baby back ribs, peeled (see Chapter 4)	1 cup water
	1 cup apple cider vinegar

1 Coat ribs with rub and let stand at least 3 hours and as long as overnight.

2 Place ribs in large pan with water and vinegar.

3 Wrap pan with foil.

4 Place pan in a smoker or on a grill, using indirect heat (see Chapter 2) to cook the ribs at 275 degrees for 3 to 4 hours. (You can also accomplish this step in an oven.)

5 Remove ribs from pan and finish directly on grill with the barbecue sauce of your choice. (Check out Chapter 9 for ideas.)

Stink-Eye Pulled Pork

James Caldwell sells his Stink-Eye BBQ Sauce in several states. He's not giving up *that* recipe, but he is sharing his pulled pork rub, which of course he shamelessly recommends serving with Stink-Eye BBQ Sauce.

Preparation time: *25 minutes plus 30 minutes cooling time*

Cooking time: *7 to 9 hours (mostly in a slow cooker, unattended)*

Yield: *6 to 8 servings*

½ cup brown sugar, packed tightly	½ teaspoon Old Bay Seasoning
3 tablespoons kosher salt	½ teaspoon thyme
1 tablespoon chili powder	½ teaspoon onion powder
½ teaspoon ground black pepper	½ teaspoon garlic powder
½ teaspoon cayenne pepper	

1 Combine all ingredients in a large mixing bowl.

2 Stir or shake to mix. Use immediately or store in an airtight container.

Pulled Pork

1 pork shoulder, about 8 pounds	Stink-Eye BBQ Sauce, or other barbecue sauce of your choice

1 Rub the pork shoulder with all the dry rub, on top and bottom of the shoulder.

2 Place pork shoulder in a 5-quart or larger slow cooker on low heat. Add ½ cup water in the bottom of the slow cooker to prevent burning.

3 Cover and cook 6 to 8 hours.

4 Check meat temperature every hour thereafter until it reaches 170 degrees.

5 Remove from slow cooker.

6 Place in a roasting pan in a preheated 500-degree oven. If you can pull out the ceramic insert from your slow cooker, skip the roasting pan and put the insert onto a cookie sheet and place both in the oven.

7 Cook 15 minutes.

8 Remove meat from oven and let rest 30 minutes.

9 Pull meat apart with forks.

10 Serve with Stink-Eye BBQ Sauce or other barbecue sauce of your choice.

Have Pizza Stone, Will Smoke Calzone

Barbecue competitions usually include an "anything but" category wherein teams vie for bragging rights over dishes that don't fit into the main judging categories — ribs, brisket, pork shoulder, and chicken. The calzone (a filled pizza crust shaped more or less into a turnover) in this chapter is a dish that qualified as "anything but."

Grilled Calzone

The Smokin' T's team says this recipe is further evidence that you shouldn't stop shopping for things to cook on the grill at the meat aisle — bread, vegetables, pizza, fruit, and so on are fair game.

Preparation time: _45 minutes (includes rising time)_

Cooking time: _30 hours_

Yield: _2 large calzones, about 6 to 8 servings_

Special equipment: _Pizza stone_

Calzone Dough

1 cup warm water

1 package active dry yeast

2 tablespoons olive oil

½ teaspoon salt

2½ cups flour

_1_ Combine water and yeast in a bowl.

_2_ Let mixture rest for 5 minutes.

_3_ Stir oil, salt, and 1½ cups of the flour into water-yeast mixture.

_4_ Add remaining flour, kneading until dough is smooth, not sticky.

_5_ Remove dough and place in a lightly greased bowl.

_6_ Let dough rise for an hour or until it has doubled in size.

_7_ Punch dough down and divide it into two portions.

_8_ Cover dough and let rest 20 minutes.

Calzone Filling

1 tablespoon olive oil

1 pound Italian sausage, loose or without casing

½ cup chopped onion

½ cup chopped green bell pepper

1 cup ricotta cheese

1 cup cubed or shredded mozzarella

½ cup grated Parmesan or Romano cheese

2 teaspoon chopped fresh sage (or ¾ teaspoon dried)

½ teaspoon black pepper

1 large egg

1 Preheat smoker or grill (using indirect heat — see Chapter 2) to 450 to 500 degrees, and set a pizza stone on the grate.

2 Heat oil in skillet at medium-high heat and brown the sausage. Set aside.

3 Using the skillet you cooked the sausage in, sauté the onion and green bell pepper for 5 minutes. Remove from heat.

4 Press each dough ball into a 12-inch circle on a piece of parchment paper or foil.

5 Combine cheeses, sage, black pepper, and egg in a large bowl.

6 Add sausage, green bell pepper, and onion, and mix well.

7 Place half of the filling onto one side of each dough circle.

8 Fold dough over to make a half-circle, and crimp the edges to seal.

9 Using a fork, poke several holes in each calzone.

10 Slide the calzones onto a pizza stone, making sure no edges hang over the edge of the stone, which would cause the crust to burn.

11 Cook 15 to 20 minutes, or until golden brown. Remove carefully.

Tip: If you prefer smaller serving sizes, you can divide the dough into three or four portions rather than just two, and press them into smaller circles accordingly.

Stylish Recipes for Lamb and Beef

Throwing burgers or steaks onto the grill is an experience most people have had and a starting point for even timid outdoor cooks. In this section, you find still-simple recipes that go at least a step beyond the "meat on grill" formula, making use of rubs and marinades.

Lamb usually isn't marbled as heavily as beef is, so what you want to look for when you buy lamb chops is a layer of smooth, white fat around the edge. *Mutton* is the name for meat from older sheep and has a much stronger, gamier flavor (probably the one that people who say they don't like lamb associate with the stuff) than the meat from young lambs.

Tuscan-Style Lamb Chops

This recipe from the Porkrastinators team gives you an easy formula for a great-tasting lamb dish.

Preparation time: *15 minutes*

Cooking time: *25 minutes*

Yield: *2 to 4 servings*

1 cup good-quality olive oil	*Juice of 1 lemon (preferably a grilled lemon)*
1 tablespoon chopped fresh garlic	
1 tablespoon chopped fresh oregano	*Kosher salt and fresh ground black pepper, to taste*
1 tablespoon chopped fresh rosemary	
1 tablespoon chopped fresh thyme	*2 racks of lamb chops*
	1 lemon, cut into wedges

1 Combine olive oil, garlic, fresh herbs, lemon juice, salt, and pepper.

2 Use additional salt and pepper to season lamb liberally.

3 Over medium-high heat, grill lamb to desired doneness, approximately 5 minutes per side, or until internal temperature reaches 125 degrees (for medium rare).

4 Remove lamb from heat and place in a small baking dish.

5 Pour oil-herb mixture over meat.

6 Cover with foil and allow to rest for 5 to 7 minutes.

7 Section racks into single chops.

8 Spoon lamb drippings and marinade over chops, and serve with grilled lemon wedges.

Beef Tenderloin with Cascabel Chile Aioli Marinade

A Cascabel chile is a small, globe-shaped number that packs a tangy, low to medium-hot punch. Paul Kirk adds Cascabels to a light-flavored, refreshing aioli.

Preparation time: _20 minutes_

Cooking time: _35 minutes_

Yield: _6 to 8 servings_

3½ pounds beef tenderloin, trimmed	1 shallot, minced
Salt	2 teaspoons red wine vinegar
Fresh ground black pepper	1 teaspoon fresh lime juice
1 Cascabel chile, stemmed, seeded, and cut into large pieces	¼ teaspoon paprika
	¼ teaspoon ancho chile powder
¾ cup mayonnaise	¼ teaspoon cayenne
1 large garlic clove, minced	2 tablespoons vegetable oil

_1_ Preheat oven to 450 degrees.

_2_ Place roasting pan on stove and heat oil over medium-high heat.

_3_ Pat tenderloin with paper towels.

_4_ Sprinkle all over with salt and pepper.

_5_ Place in roasting pan with oil and roast in oven (or in a hot, covered grill).

_6_ While meat cooks, toast Cascabel chile in a small skillet over high heat, turning pieces once, until blistered and fragrant.

_7_ Let cool until brittle.

_8_ Using a mortar and pestle, pound chile into a powder.

_9_ Mix powder in medium bowl with remaining ingredients to create the aioli.

_10_ Remove meat from oven or grill after 25 to 30 minutes, or when internal temperature is in the 130- to 150-degree range. Because you're using such a hot oven, you may want to check the internal temperature of the meat as the 25-minute mark approaches to make sure you don't overcook it.

_11_ Let rest 10 to 15 minutes

_12_ Slice and serve with aioli on the side.

Italian Espresso Steak

Brandon Hamilton concocted this recipe for the java lovers of the world. The coffee flavor in the rub isn't overbearing, and the other seasonings pair nicely with the coffee overtones.

Preparation time: *15 minutes, plus 1 hour resting time*

Cooking time: *About 15 minutes, depending on desired doneness*

Yield: *4 servings*

2-pound beef strip loin, trimmed	*2 teaspoons brown sugar*
4 tablespoons finely ground espresso coffee beans	*1 teaspoon dry mustard powder*
3 tablespoons chili powder	*2 teaspoons fresh ground black pepper*
1 tablespoon granulated garlic	*1 bunch green onions, sliced (optional)*
2 teaspoons kosher salt	*1 lemon, cut into 8 wedges (optional)*

1 Cut the cleaned strip loin into 4-ounce portions, about 1 inch thick.

2 In a small bowl, combine the remaining ingredients.

3 Press the rub generously on the beef steaks. Discard any remaining seasoning mixture.

4 Place steaks in a glass dish; cover and refrigerate 1 hour.

5 Preheat the grill to a medium temperature.

6 Place seasoned steaks onto grill uncovered, 8 to 10 minutes or until desired doneness, turning occasionally.

7 Serve steaks sliced on an angle; garnish with green onions and lemon wedges, if you like.

Korean Beef Barbecue (Bulgogi)

Brandon Hamilton offers this recipe, which gives you a super-simple way to grill beef that produces a striking result.

Preparation time: *15 minutes, plus marinating time*

Cooking time: *About 5 minutes*

Yield: *4 servings*

2-pound top sirloin steak, trimmed	1 teaspoon sesame oil
2 tablespoons molasses	3 garlic cloves, minced
6 tablespoons low-sodium soy sauce	1 teaspoon ground black pepper
1½ tablespoons rice vinegar	

1 Clean the excess fat from the beef and slice diagonally against the grain into 2-inch-thick slices.

2 In a resealable plastic bag, combine all ingredients. Seal the bag securely, making sure to remove the excess air from the bag.

3 Marinate the beef in the refrigerator 1 to 2 hours, rotating the bag occasionally to ensure that all the beef is covered in marinade.

4 Preheat the grill to 350 degrees.

5 Gently remove the beef from the marinade and transfer directly to the grill. Make sure to place the slices of beef against the grain of the grill grate.

6 Grill the beef for approximately 5 minutes (about 2 minutes per side) or until desired doneness.

Traditionally, the meat for bulgogi is sliced almost paper thin, which is no mean feat unless you have a meat slicer. Keeping the slices thicker also enables you to cook it on the grill, adding an extra layer of flavor.

Bulgogi often is served in lettuce leaves, but it tastes great with rice, too.

Pork Satay

Paul Kirk draws from Southeast Asian cooking tradition for this simple and savory recipe.

Preparation time: *15 minutes, plus marinade overnight*

Cooking time: *15 minutes*

Yield: *4 servings*

Special equipment: *Metal or bamboo skewers, soaked in water*

½ cup unsweetened coconut milk

2 large garlic cloves, minced

2 tablespoons finely chopped cilantro

2 tablespoons peanut oil

1 tablespoon brown sugar

1 tablespoon soy sauce

1 teaspoon fresh ground black pepper

1 pound lean pork loin, sliced ¼-inch think and cut into 3-x-¾-inch strips

Lettuce leaves

1 Combine first seven ingredients.

2 Pour into large freezer bag and add pork pieces.

3 Refrigerate at least 2 hours and as long as overnight.

4 Thread strips on skewers and grill over medium-hot fire about 3 minutes per skewer, depending on the thickness of the strips.

5 Serve with lettuce leaves.

Chapter 14

Great Dishes for Leftover Barbecue

*B*arbecue takes work, which in many cases means that if you're going to make it, you're going to make a whole lot of it. That way your efforts are rewarded over more than one night's dinner, but the downside is that your fridge may end up too full of pork shoulder, brisket, or chicken.

The conundrum is one that anyone who's ever cooked a turkey knows well and is the basis for a thousand permutations of turkey casserole.

Fortunately, barbecue starts out with more flavor than most interpretations of the illustrious holiday bird, so the methods for utilizing leftovers produce some awfully tasty results, not to mention the epic Spudzilla. You find the recipe for the monster potato and other creative ways for utilizing leftovers in the pages to come.

Crafting Dishes That Stick to Tradition

Like peanut butter and chocolate or Hall and Oates, certain things just go together. Nobody would be surprised to find baked beans at a barbecue, for example, or to see potatoes coming into play in one form or another.

The recipes in this section give you some tasty new ways to pair ingredients that have a history.

Competition Pit Beans

Seth McAllister of Team Porkrastinators calls this an easy recipe but warns that the canned beans tend to be sweet. Cut back on the sugar for a more savory version. McAllister also advises smoking the beans with hickory, which is a great complement to the flavors in the dish.

Preparation time: *10 minutes*

Cooking time: *25 minutes*

Yield: *10 to 12 servings*

¼ cup rendered brisket fat or ½ stick butter

1 yellow onion, diced

3 cloves garlic

1 teaspoon black pepper

28-ounce can Bush's Original Baked Beans

28-ounce can Bush's Boston Beans

28-ounce can Bush's Boston Beans, drained

1½ tablespoons dry rub (see Chapter 6)

1 tablespoon Dijon mustard

1 cup sweet barbecue sauce (see Chapter 9)

1 pound leftover barbecue meat

1 cup dark brown sugar

1 In a large pot, melt brisket fat or butter over medium-high heat.

2 If you're using brisket fat, remove any chunks that didn't render.

3 Turn the heat to high and add onion, garlic, and pepper.

4 Sauté until lightly browned.

5 Turn heat to medium-low and let the mixture sweat until the onion has softened.

6 Add the beans, rub, mustard, and barbecue sauce, and stir thoroughly.

7 Simmer over low heat until the beans have warmed through, about 5 minutes.

8 Remove from heat and stir in the meat.

9 Sprinkle brown sugar on top of the beans, but do not stir it in.

10 Place the pot on the smoker and smoke at 225 to 250 degrees for 2 hours.

11 Remove beans from smoker and stir in brown sugar.

Tip: *If you don't want to bust out the smoker, you can accomplish roughly the same results by cooking the dish in a large Dutch oven. Add ½ teaspoon of liquid smoke (see Chapter 8) if you want to make sure you get the smoke flavor. It also works just fine if you cook it in a slow cooker for 6 to 8 hours.*

Spudzilla

The brains behind Spudzilla run TC's Memphis BBQ, a restaurant where Spudzillas fly out of the kitchen doors or, given their ample girth, are more likely wheeled out. The finished product weighs somewhere between 3 and 4 pounds, hence the name. Diners at TC's earn a T-shirt if they conquer a Spudzilla in one sitting. More reasonable folk could slice it into portions (a good four of them, no doubt) or start with smaller spuds.

Preparation time: *10 minutes*

Cooking time: *None*

Yield: *2 to 4 servings*

1 large baked potato (1 to 1 ½ pounds) or 2 or 3 smaller potatoes to equal 1 ½ pounds	1 cup barbecued pork
	½ cup baked beans
¼ cup butter	⅓ cup diced tomatoes
¼ cup sour cream	⅓ cup diced onion
1 cup nacho cheese	¼ cup canned sliced jalapeños

1 Place baked potato on a plate, cut it lengthwise and crosswise, and then mash it lightly with a fork.

2 Spread the butter and sour cream over the potato.

3 Top with nacho cheese.

4 Add warmed barbecued pork.

5 Spoon baked beans over the pork on a diagonal.

6 Finish the spud with tomatoes, onion, and jalapeños.

Baking the perfect potato

Some people swear by baking their spuds in a microwave, but those are probably the same people who think instant coffee is a great notion. To bake a nice potato — one that's soft inside and has a crispy skin, you need time and an oven. Here's how:

1. **Preheat your oven to 350 degrees.**

2. **Scrub your spuds and stab them a couple times on each side with a fork.**

3. **Brush the potatoes with olive or vegetable oil.**

4. **Place them right on the rack, with a baking sheet on the lower rack to catch the drippings.**

5. **Take them out of the oven when the skin looks browned and crinkly, and the potatoes feel soft if you squeeze them.**

For a potato as big as the one you want for Spudzilla, that means a good 90 minutes of baking.

Barbecue Hash

More than a fine use for leftover barbecue, Paul Kirk's barbecue hash is comfort in a casserole pan.

Preparation time: 10 minutes

Cooking time: 30 minutes

Yield: 4 to 6 servings

2 cups cold barbecue brisket or pulled pork

1 cup cold cooked potatoes, diced

½ cup diced onions

⅓ cup diced green bell pepper

1 cup canned or leftover gravy

Salt and pepper, to taste

¼ cup breadcrumbs

¼ cup grated cheddar cheese

1 tablespoon butter

Paprika, to taste

1 Preheat oven to 350 degrees.

2 Butter a 2-quart casserole pan.

3 Combine brisket or pork, potatoes, onions, bell pepper, gravy, salt, and pepper.

4 Place in buttered casserole pan.

5 Sprinkle with breadcrumbs and cheese.

6 Dot with butter, and sprinkle with paprika.

7 Bake until cheese is melted and casserole is warm throughout, about 30 minutes.

Jalapeño Shot Shells

The Smoke Hunters team makes use of its leftover brisket with this crowd-pleasing snack or side dish.

Preparation time: *15 minutes*

Cooking time: *30 minutes*

Yield: *6 servings*

6 large jalapeño peppers	*½ cup leftover brisket*
½ cup cream cheese	*½ pound thick-cut bacon*
¼ cup Smoke Hunters' BBQ Rub (see Chapter 6)	

1 Slice peppers in half and clean out membrane and seeds.

2 Fill each with a small scoop of cream cheese.

3 Dust cream cheese with rub.

4 Pile on a forkful of cooked shredded brisket.

5 Wrap each with a half piece of bacon, and hold together with a toothpick.

6 Place peppers on a smoker or grill until outside of pepper is roasted.

Tip: *You can get similar results without fighting the melty cream cheese by baking this dish in a 350-degree oven for about 30 minutes.*

The jalapeño gamble

Can you tell how hot a pepper is going to be just by looking? Depends on who you ask. So many factors go into a pepper's heat level (which is based on how much capsaicin it contains), that there really is no easy way to figure out just by looking or touching how hot a pepper is going to taste.

The capsaicin comes from the *placenta,* the middle, white material inside a pepper that holds the seeds. Capsaicin may leak into the seeds, but it doesn't originate in them, as many people think. If you taste a pepper and find it has more punch than you care for, scrape away more of the pithy inner tissue, and you scrape away much of the heat.

It may be an urban legend, but some people insist that you can determine how hot a jalapeño is going to be by its shape. Rounder is milder, the lore has it, so pick a pointy-ended jalapeño if you're looking for the burn.

Culture Combos: Using Barbecue Leftovers in Unexpected Ways

Apple pie didn't get its start in America, no matter what well-worn similes may tell you. Apple pie got its start in Europe. Barbecue, on the other hand, may well be the only form of distinctly American cuisine.

If the recipes that follow are any indication, that means its ripe for combining with a little something from elsewhere.

Big R's Smoked BBQ Spaghetti

This recipe from the Smoke Hunters team uses hot links, a kind of spicy sausage that's a staple in Texas barbecue.

Preparation time: *25 minutes*

Cooking time: *20 minutes*

Yield: *6 to 8 servings*

1-pound box spaghetti

¼ cup Smoke Hunters' BBQ Rub (see Chapter 6)

4 smoked hot links, cut into ½-inch-thick slices

½ pound smoked pork butt

1 cup barbecue sauce

1 Cook spaghetti according to package instructions.

2 Place cooked spaghetti in medium foil pan.

3 Dust with Smoke Hunters' BBQ Rub.

4 Add hot links, smoked pork, and barbecue sauce.

5 Place pan in a 225-degree barbecue pit for 20 minutes.

BBQ Fried Rice

Dan Cannon, the cook behind BBQ by Dan (www.bbqbydan.com) uses this recipe for leftover barbecue meat of any form or combination.

Preparation time: *25 minutes*

Cooking time: *40 minutes*

Yield: *5 to 6 servings*

2 cups uncooked rice (this makes 4½ cups cooked rice)

3 eggs

1 tablespoon butter

½ cup diced onion

1 cup barbecue meats (your choice: brisket, butt, chicken, pork, or rib meat, or a combination thereof)

½ cup shredded smoked brisket

2 to 4 tablespoons vegetable oil

¼ to ½ cup soy sauce

1 cup frozen peas and carrots

Salt and pepper, to taste

1 Cook rice according to package instructions.

2 In a small pan, scramble eggs over medium heat. Set aside.

3 In an oversized cast iron fry pan, melt butter over medium heat.

4 Add onions and cook until translucent.

5 Add all barbecue meat and cook until almost browned.

6 Add ¼ cup vegetable oil.

7 Spoon in rice, while stirring, until you've blended all of it into the butter, onions, and meat.

8 Continue to stir, and add additional ¼ cup oil if you need it.

9 Stir in ¼ cup soy sauce and stir until all the rice becomes brown.

10 Add another ¼ cup soy sauce to bring mixture to desired texture, color, and taste.

11 Stir in peas, carrots, and eggs, and mix thoroughly.

12 Continue stirring until vegetables are heated through.

13 Add salt and pepper to taste.

Variation: *For a drier rice that works particularly well with this recipe, Dan recommends parboiling the rice, which means boiling it only partway before adding it to the recipe. To parboil, simply cook the rice for about 3/4 of the time that the package instructions call for, rinse it in cold water, and then drain it. It'll cook further as you mix it with the other ingredients in the pan, eventually coming to the same degree of doneness that it would have through boiling and without going past its ideal, firm state.*

Part V
The Part of Tens

"You can clean up before company arrives, but use the shower, not the bathtub–I'm marinating the steaks."

In this part . . .

More morsel than meal, each chapter in this part offers quick hits of information. You find ten common mistakes so you don't have to make them yourself and ten bits of critical barbecue wisdom straight from the horses' mouths. I give you ten great sources for more information about barbecue techniques, equipment, recipes, and a whole lot more, as well as ten places to kick up your heels or pit your cooking skills against competitors at a barbecue festival.

Chapter 15

Ten Ways Rookies Ruin Good Meat

*Y*ou will make mistakes as you find your footing in barbecue cooking. If you don't, you're probably not trying anything new. Mistakes are part of the adventure, but they aren't so much the tasty part.

In this chapter, I direct you away from ten mistakes that many people before you have made. The advice in this chapter comes from centuries of other people figuring out the hard way, and it frees you up to walk a smoother path to delicious barbecue, as well as to invent some new mistakes all your own.

Being in an All-Fired Hurry

If you want fast, cook a grilled cheese. If you want barbecue, chill out. *Slow* is the essence of barbecue. Cooking at low temperatures for a goodly amount of time is what makes barbecue barbecue and makes the meat melt in your mouth. Before you cook, put some thought into how much time you're going to need, how you want to season or sauce your product, and the sides you want to serve with it. Planning ahead makes you less likely to get distracted when your meat needs you most.

The prep work you do before you even get the meat near the heat keeps it tender and gives it your unique touch of flavor. Why rush past the prep or try to hurry the cooking? Savor the process as you will savor the product.

Sprinting Past Your Experience Level

Barbecue creates converts faster than the smoothest-talking tele-vangelist, but you're better off letting your enthusiasm simmer before you take on intense barbecue projects for a party of friends and family. You may be eager to show off your new bullet smoker, but don't let your mouth make promises your barbecue can't keep.

Barbecue comes with a lot of variables, and although most of what you do will become second nature after you get the swing of things, you have a lot to keep track of in the beginning. Better to take it slow, making subtle changes in your recipes or processes, than to rush ahead and bring frustration to your table.

Using Wood Before Its Time

When you cook over wood, the flavor of the smoke that rises from the chips or chunks of hickory or oak or whatever seeps its way through your meat. Given the cooking time you're investing, that's a lot of flavor, so it'd better be a good one. Using wood that hasn't been aged properly is a sure way to throw off your flavor, and in some cases the texture of your meat — some green woods blacken meat, and that's because creosote is abundant in fresh wood (and light in aged wood).

Freshly cut wood has a lot of moisture, which means a lot of smoke — and oversmoking overpowers the natural flavor of the meat and can make it taste bitter.

Because the wood chips or chunks provide a flavor source rather than a heat source, you don't want to burn them. A solid soak in cool water keeps them moist enough that they slowly release smoke. Shoot for half an hour to an hour of soaking time.

Taking Meat from Fridge to Fire

Temperature being one of the gods of great barbecue, you want to keep a handle on the temperature of your meat as well as that of your smoker. Putting meat onto the grate right from the refrigerator adds a lot of cold air to your smoker, and that's likely to lead to condensation of creosote from the charcoal. The creosote floats up via the smoke and onto your meat, adding a flavor and texture that's probably not what you're after.

Let your meat sit at room temperature for about an hour before you cook it. Most recipes count on your doing so and advise cooking times that are based on the meat starting at about room temperature.

Letting meat rest at room temperature for more than an hour is a bad idea. When it gets too warm, it also becomes susceptible to bacteria.

Lighting Charcoal with Lighter Fluid

If you drink naphtha for breakfast and chase it with benzene, by all means, coat your charcoal with lighter fluid before you light it. You'll enjoy the acrid tang the flammables impart to your brisket. If you'd rather taste the sweetness of the apple wood you smoked it over and the bite of your rub, skip the lighter fluid and use a chimney starter instead. You can find them at just about any hardware store, and they enable you to skip the lighter fluid. All you need is the charcoal, some paper, and a match. I tell you about using a chimney starter in Chapter 2.

A chimney starter comes in handy when you want to add more charcoal to increase the heat in your smoker. Get the charcoals going first in the chimney instead of throwing them in cold. Doing so gives you better control over your heat and lets any odors in the briquettes burn off before they have a chance to waft up into your meat.

Overcorrecting, Overzealously

A steady temperature is kindest to your meat, meaning it'll be kindest to your tongue when all's said and done. Fluctuating temperatures make for uneven cooking and can dry out your meat. Adding heat is always easier than reducing it, so start conservatively, erring on the side of too little charcoal and slowly adding more briquettes as you need them.

Keep your eye on the temperature with a good thermometer, and keep the lid on your smoker as much as possible. Peeking in is tempting, but it's the enemy of a steady temperature.

Load up the grate with meat, and you may think the answer is to add more heat to cook it. Stop right there. More heat is just going to dry out your product and may even burn it. Instead, remove some of the meat to allow air to flow throughout the unit and keep the temperature steady throughout the smoker.

Getting Sauced Early

Sugar has low heat tolerance. So do tomatoes. These two mainstays of barbecue sauces are the very things that give your chicken a black, crackling coating if you try to cook with them. The chicken (or any other meat) takes longer to cook than does the sauce, which burns right around it. Wait until you're almost finished cooking before you add a sweet sauce with tomatoes. A minute or two on each side of the meat over a low to moderate flame is all the time the sauce needs to add taste and texture.

If you prefer to baste the meat while it cooks, use a sauce with a low sugar content or one that you've thinned with water or vinegar.

Relying on Eyes, Not Numbers

Your eyes may deceive you when it comes to figuring out whether your meat is cooked. This is particularly true when you smoke meat because smoked chicken and pork tend to pink as they cook instead of taking on the white color that reassures cooks and eaters that the meat has been thoroughly cooked.

Find meat's internal temperature to determine whether it's ready for sampling. Chapter 4 gives you a rundown of the internal temperatures you want to reach for different cuts of meat.

Poking Holes into the Meat

You want to keep the precious juices inside the meat, so use tongs anytime you move it. Stab it and you provide a sure route for the juices to ooze out, taking with them any hope you had for great barbecue.

Forgetting Rest Time

The hours of preparation behind you, the cooking complete at long last, pulling apart your pork shoulder is quite a temptation. Do so too soon, and you throw out all your hard work in an instant.

Meat's juices go where the heat is lowest, so give them a chance at your cutting board, and they run for it. If, instead, you let the meat rest after you take it off the heat, the juices have a chance to be reabsorbed by the proteins that set them free in the first place. Cut into a well-rested piece of meat, and you find tender juiciness rather than a puddle around your desiccated pork chop. Chapter 4 gives you the specifics about letting meat rest.

Chapter 16

Ten Truer Words Were Never Spoken

*B*arbecue became a sport for good reason, and part of that is because barbecue cooks tend toward the competitive and opinionated. Each recipe and each fine-tuning of this or that cooking technique is held by someone to be *the* critical element of his or her barbecue success.

In this chapter, I give you ten points about barbecue that everyone can agree on.

The Truth Is in the Cook, Not the Equipment

You find advantages to higher-end smokers, the ones that keep a steady temperature as long as you need them to and do everything but give you a backrub while your pork shoulder cooks. But do you need them? Nah.

Just consider the origins of barbecue: The culinary tradition that we now call hobby and follow as sport started out of necessity, with people who had very little in the way of resources. They cooked the worst cuts of meat in holes they dug in the ground, and in doing so, they stumbled onto some great science and created an enduring cuisine.

True enough — top-of-the-line equipment makes cooking easier. But at its heart, barbecue is a way to get around the need for expensive paraphernalia. And although new, shiny, technically enhanced cookers are tempting and marketers will assure you that they're even necessary, all you need is almost nothing.

Cook Low and Slow

What went down in underprivileged, rural areas — by necessity and by trial and error — has some hard science behind it. When you cook meat slowly, over low heat, hydrolysis occurs.

Hydrolysis means that the tight collagen fibers in the tendons are interrupted by molecules of water from the moist heat and from elsewhere in the muscle tissue. The tough collagen becomes soft gelatin, and the meat becomes tender. Voilà!

Hydrolysis takes place only at relatively low cooking temperatures. You don't get the same reaction when you sear meat on a grill or griddle.

If You're Lookin', You're Not Cookin'

Playwright Oscar Wilde said he could resist anything but temptation, and for most rookie barbecue cooks, the temptation to take just a peek at what's going on inside the smoker is too much to resist.

Resist. For the love of brisket, resist.

When you open your smoker to eyeball your meat, you gain nothing but the satisfaction of knowing that a very unlikely rib robbery hasn't taken place in your backyard. Plus, you harm what's there.

Maintaining a steady temperature throughout the smoker is the best way to produce evenly cooked, tender meat. Open the smoker and you throw the temperature balance out of whack, create hot and cool spots, and usually lose several degrees along the way. You abuse your good ingredients and all the care you've put into the product. And for what? Everything you need to know is in the temperature and the timing.

There Is Such a Thing as Oversmoking

The smoke that wafts up from whatever wood you use in your smoker cushions the meat you cook from the direct heat of the charcoal below and infuses it with subtle flavors. It's a big part of what makes barbecue barbecue, but too much of it makes barbecue inedible.

You can get a bitter smoke flavor from using too much wood in your cooker. The surest way to avoid that is to add small amounts of wood to the smoker over a long period of time rather than a whole heap at the start. And if it's heat you're looking for, make sure that you add charcoal instead of wood.

Sauce on the Side, Nothing to Hide

Although many barbecue eaters (and even some cooks) equate the whole of barbecue with the sauce, ideally even the best sauce serves only to complement well-prepared meat.

Any barbecue meat that has been adeptly prepared and cooked stands without a lick of sauce. On the flip side of that, sauce is like a barbecue muumuu, something bold and big used to hide what the cook doesn't want you to see — overcooked or oversmoked meat, a flavorless preparation, or a past-its-prime cut.

Sauce is a great part of the barbecue equation and a great way to experiment, but it's not the be-all and end-all. You have to have a foundation of great meat before you can boast your barbecue prowess.

Hot Dogs and Hamburgers Are Not Barbecue

Not that there's anything wrong with hot dogs and hamburgers. Just please don't confuse them with barbecue. Barbecue takes place slowly, over low heat in a closed cooking apparatus with smoke from aged wood.

Grilling is what you do with steaks or weenies. It involves high heat and quick cooking. It's good stuff, but it isn't barbecue. When you grill, you typically use different cuts of meat and cook them by a completely different technique. The only similarity, really, is that you cook by either method outdoors. Oh, and you use charcoal either way.

Refer to grilling as "barbecuing," and you're going to raise hackles in a hurry.

Time Is on Your Side

Never has patience been so beautifully rewarded as when you sink your teeth into a perfect pulled-pork sandwich that you babied from rub to rest time.

Timing your barbecue project is critical for getting the result you want. Make sure you allow plenty of time for preparation and cooking, and keep notes of your cooking exploits so that you can best narrow down the cook times that give you the best end product.

Meat That Falls Off the Bone Has Been Cooked Too Long

Fall-off-the-bone tender usually is used as a term of endearment when applied to barbecued ribs, but meat that literally falls from the bone is overcooked.

What you want to shoot for is meat that pulls cleanly from the bone. You want to "bite 'em, not fight 'em," and the bite part of that equation means you don't want the ribs to be something you don't need teeth for. Texture is an important part of the deal when it comes to ribs.

Watch for meat that shrinks away from the ends of the bones (about ¼ inch to ½ inch at the most). That's a good indication that it's ready to come away from the heat.

Cleanliness Is Next to Tastiness

Buildup on your cooking grate can impart some unwelcome flavors on your barbecue meats. And a grunged-up grate is sticky — it'll grab whatever you're cooking and hold it, meaning you leave food on the grate or pick up remnants from the chicken you cooked three weeks ago.

Clean your grate with a wire brush after you've heated it up but before you put anything on it, and clean it again after you're done cooking. Have at it while you let your meat rest. (Turn to Chapter 4 to find out about meat's much-needed rest after cooking.)

Fat Is Flavor

This is a hard one to drive home, given the current nutritional climate, in which fat has become such a villain that it practically wears a black cape and twirls a handlebar moustache.

Quite simply: Fat is flavor, especially when it comes to barbecue cooking, which relies on the slow breakdown of fat to add moisture and tang to whatever you're cooking.

Fat serves as storage, and that means that the flavors of the animal's diet stick around in the fat cells. As I tell you in Chapter 5, smell has more to do with taste than anything that happens on your tongue, and fat holds most of the aroma-producing molecules, meaning that it lets loose a lot of good scents that you read as taste.

Look for meat that has heavy, even marbling to get the most flavor out of your barbecue cooking. Don't be afraid to apply rub to the fat on the meat — it'll infuse that flavor, too.

Chapter 17

Ten (Or So) Places to Turn for Tips

In This Chapter
- ▶ Leaning on more experienced cooks
- ▶ Hooking up with a mentor organization
- ▶ Finding inspiration and education

*B*arbecue incites passion, and fortunately the passionate aren't shy about sharing opinions and advice. Most are happy to help bring a novice into the fold.

In this chapter, I direct you to a few of the hundreds of places you can turn to find out more about barbecue cooking. Most of these resources also serve as starting points, connecting you to further opportunities to nurture your barbecue habit.

Kansas City Barbeque Society

The sanctioning body for hundreds of competitions across the country each year, Kansas City Barbeque Society (KCBS) bills itself as "the world's largest organization of barbecue and grilling enthusiasts."

KCBS was set up in 1986 to celebrate and support barbecue cooking in all its forms (especially cooking as sport — one of its major endeavors is training judges and overseeing competitions). The organization offers cooking classes throughout the year in a slew of locations, and produces a monthly newsletter, *The Bullsheet*, which is full of news and information about equipment, techniques, and contest updates.

Find out more about Kansas City Barbeque Society at www.kcbs.us.

National Barbecue Association

Sprouted in North Carolina in 1991 and settled in Texas since 2001, the National Barbecue Association (NBBQA) set out to bring together all sides of the barbecue industry and story. It conducts industry research, culls recipes and tips from pros, sanctions competitions, certifies judges, and brings everyone together each year at a rollicking conference.

A member directory helps connect all stripes of industry insiders and home cooks, and a quarterly magazine for all NBBQA members offers tips about running and promoting a barbecue business, as well as tips and recipes for the hobbyist.

On the NBBQA Web site (www.nbbqa.org), you can find a slew of resources for advice and recipes.

The North Carolina Barbecue Society

Hailing from one of the country's hotbeds of barbecue, The North Carolina Barbecue Society (NCBS) is a recent but hotheaded addition to the country's barbecue associations. With a chapped hide from others' having beaten it to the punch, this organization wants to refocus barbecue to North Carolina, promoting the state's history, culture, cuisine, and agriculture along the way.

What the group lacks in history it more than makes up for in fire . . . and dedication: The society's Web site (www.ncbbqsociety.com) is an easy-to-navigate home for recipes, news, event information, classes (within the state), and a goodly amount of links to other sites. The NCBS sends out a bimonthly newsletter, *Pig Tales,* and has organized a "barbecue trail" that guides visitors through some of the state's best offerings.

The Virtual Weber Bullet

Put together by fans of the popular smoker rather than by the company that makes it, this site (www.virtualweberbullet.com) is an amazingly thorough collection of information about everything barbecue. On it, you find detailed sections about operating the smoker after which the site is named (the Weber Smokey Mountain Cooker, commonly known as the *bullet smoker*), other sections about selecting and cooking various meats, and still others filled with articles providing barbecue and other cooking wisdom.

Recipes abound on the site and give you formulas for everything from brisket to brined salmon, baked apples to focaccia. Forums contain ongoing discussions of thousands of topics. Log in to get answers to almost every possible question, and opinions on matters you hadn't thought to question yet.

So comprehensive is the site that a monthly e-newsletter keeps subscribers up-to-date about the most recent 30 days' worth of additions.

The Smoke Ring

The Smoke Ring brings together all the barbecue- and grilling-related Web sites whose Webmasters invested the three minutes necessary to sign up. You get a lot of great information from the ring, but you sift through some chaff to get there.

The ring's home page (www.thesmokering.com) enables you to browse its 1,000-plus member sites one by one or to search for key words on those sites. Wanna buy a used propane-powered offset horizontal smoker? Whip up a Creole-influenced rub for your chicken? Type your desire into the search box and find opinions and options.

A contest calendar, cookbook reviews, news, articles, lively forums, and a recipe section accessed right from the ring's home page make the site worth visiting. If you have the time, a random site link button leads to some interesting (and unexpected) information.

The Barbeque Forum

In 1995, the Barbeque Forum (www.thebbqforum.com), broke new ground as the first online forum about barbecue. Only 60 messages were posted that year. Now hundreds are posted in a single day.

As the name suggests, the forum and the opportunity it provides to pick the brains of experienced barbecue cooks is the main reason for visiting The Barbeque Forum, but you find many more: links to podcasts, classifieds where you can unload or purchase equipment, and a blog co-written sporadically by a number of contributors.

Barbecue'n on the Internet

Easy to navigate and full of advice for the beginner, Barbecue'n on the Internet (www.barbecuen.com) contains article after article, many of them on an "According to Smoky" page that features seemingly unlimited wisdom from C. Clark "Smoky" Hale, a barbecue authority of long standing and the author of *The Great American Barbecue & Grilling Manual* (Abacus Publishing).

Sections on equipment, charcoal, and spices — and a complete beginners' guide — set the site apart. Information on the site goes deep. You even find a section devoted to articles about spices, wherein expert Ann Wilder covers the nuances among sugars and the uses for Szechuan peppers, among other things.

An enormous recipe collection will keep you cooking for the foreseeable future; the site's barbecue store connects you to everything you need to cook in the first place.

Further Regional Barbecue Associations

If you're looking for a closer-to-home congregation of barbecue enthusiasts, chances are good you have a barbecue association in your neighborhood, if not your backyard. Barbecue cooking has infiltrated even areas known more for clam chowder than smoked brisket, and as its popularity grows, so does the number of organizations dedicated to spreading the gospel.

Here are a few of the well-established organizations, from one end of the United States to the other:

✔ Arizona BBQ Association (www.azbbqa.com)

✔ California Barbecue Association (www.cbbqa.org)

✔ Central Texas Barbecue Association (www.ctbbqa.org)

✔ Greater Omaha Barbecue Society (www.gobs.org)

✔ Florida Barbecue Association (www.flbbq.org)

✔ Illinois BBQ Society (www.ilbbqs.com)

✔ Iowa Barbeque Society (www.iabbq.org)

✔ Memphis in May (www.memphisinmay.org)

✔ New England Barbecue Society (www.nebs.org)

✔ Pacific Northwest Barbecue Association (www.pnwba.com)

✔ South Carolina Barbeque Association
(www.scbarbeque.com)

✔ Texas Gulf Coast BBQ Cookers Association
(www.tgcbca.org)

Chapter 18

Ten World-Famous Barbecue Events

*G*iven the braggadocio that's been part and parcel of barbecue cooking maybe as long as hogs have been thrown into pits, barbecue cooking becoming sport was inevitable. Each year brings hundreds of competitions for cooks of every level, and those competitions offer the chance not just to sample great eats but to share information, maybe take some classes, and usually groove to live music.

Not every festival has a competitive element, and in this list you find a couple events that are purely for celebration of America's greatest culinary contribution.

Jack Daniel's World Championship Invitational Barbecue

The biggest of the bigs: The Jack Daniel's World Championship Invitational Barbecue is the premier barbecue cooking event. Nobody makes it into the competition without beating out at least 50 other teams in a barbecue competition, or 2 dozen other teams in a designated state championship competition. While the elite teams sweat out the competition, visitors whoop it up at the surrounding festival.

The competition takes place over two days each fall at the Jack Daniel Distillery in Lynchburg, Tennessee. Bonus: Visitors can tour the distillery during the competition.

For more information, go to www.jackdaniels.com.

Memphis in May World Championship

One full mile of barbecue competition, vending, music, and more: The Memphis in May World Championship Barbecue Cooking Contest is three days of springtime merriment — and pulled pork — that takes place in downtown Memphis, right on the bank of the Mississippi River and next to Beale Street. If you can't have fun amid all that, you're just not trying.

A People's Choice contest gives visitors a *taste* — yeah, I went there — of competition judging, and the Cooker's Caravan gives visitors behind-the-scenes looks at competition cooking and a chance to beg tips from the contestants.

For more information, go to http://memphisinmay.org/wcbcc_visitor.htm.

National BBQ Festival

Drawing winners from barbecue contests of all stripes for its Best of the Best Invitational, the National BBQ Festival annually turns Douglas, Georgia, into barbecue central.

In addition to the Best of the Best competition, cook-offs in several other categories are open and award prizes for backyard cooks, kids, and masters of sweet potato pie.

Food vendors, an antiques auction, music, and "south Georgia's largest indoor yard sale" round out the two-day event, which takes place mid-fall each year.

For more information, go to www.nationalbbqfestival.com.

American Royal Barbecue

Part of the century (and then some)–old American Royal cattle exposition, horse show, and rodeo, American Royal Barbecue draws 500 competitors to its invitational and its open competition. "Barbecuelooza" brings a Texas Hold'em tournament, a professional rodeo event, a concert series, and all manner of barbecue goodness available for the eating.

Drawing 70,000 visitors, the American Royal Barbecue started in 1980 and now bills itself as the biggest barbecue competition in the world. It happens each year during the fall in Kansas City, Kansas.

For more information, go to www.americanroyal.com.

Big Pig Jig

Originally a whole-hog cooking contest, the Big Pig Jig has grown in every way and now includes categories for Brunswick stew, ribs, sauce, and so on. The festival draws crowds of more than 20,000.

An annual event that takes place in the early fall in Vienna, Georgia, the Big Pig Jig is held in conjunction with a major arts-and-crafts fair and the local livestock association's annual hog show.

Festival events take place over the span of a week, starting with a quiz bowl and wrapping up with a concert. In between are a golf tournament, a 5K run, a hog calling contest, and food, of course.

For more information, go to www.bigpigjig.com.

Big Apple Barbecue Block Party

Two summer days of food and music hit New York's Madison Square Park for the first time in 2003, and the event took hold right away. Several big muckety-mucks of barbecue come in from all over the country to show off their skills. Big-time food gurus lead seminars on all things barbecue.

And then there's the music: Big Apple Barbecue Block Party pairs brisket with blues, providing a two-day lineup of live bands.

No competition at this one, just tons of incredible food and fun in the big city.

For more information, go to www.bigapplebbq.org.

Lakeland Pig Festival

Balmy winter fun in Lakeland, Florida, the Lakeland Pig Festival is all about the barbecue. Pros and backyard cooks compete in separate divisions, and kids have their own competition, too.

Founded in not-too-long-ago 1997, the festival quickly drew a following and now attracts 30,000 visitors. There's music, and a children's area at the festival, but the focus is on the food, and visitors can take barbecue cooking classes and even sample the efforts of the competing teams.

Best in the West Nugget Rib Cook-Off

A massive, five-day event that takes place over Labor Day, the Best in the West Nugget Rib Cook-Off draws a half-million people to Sparks, Nevada, for food, six stages of music, an arts-and-crafts show, and a rollicking kids' area.

There's judging, but this event isn't sanctioned by one of the major barbecue associations and so is more a chance to hang out in the high desert chewing some ribs and having a fine time than to witness the kind of intense competition you find at other competitions.

For more information, go to www.nuggetribcookoff.com.

LPQue BBQ Championship

A newer entrant to the competition circuit, the LPQue BBQ Championship is a summertime event held in Mt. Pleasant, Iowa. This one's unique because it's the first major competition within a new Kansas City Barbecue Society (KCBS) delineation — the

"Competitor Series" — and because it takes advantage of the series' allowing changes to the usual KCBS rules by requiring that all competitors use liquid-propane-fueled cookers.

The departure from charcoal and wood (which still are allowed, just not as the primary heat source) raised some hackles, but the event offers a heckuva prize purse (the largest in KCBS history) and draws some heavy hitters. A barbecue dinner and concert give visitors a chance to hobnob with the teams.

For more information, go to www.1pque.com.

Blue Ridge BBQ Festival

A state championship event that was introduced in 1994, the Blue Ridge BBQ Festival has the benefit of great location (at the foot of Warrior Mountain and next to the banks of Pacolet River in Tryon, North Carolina) and a great reputation that draws healthy competition.

Two days of food, competition, arts, music, and carnival rides for the kiddies were a must for the summer festival. Going green was a unique initiative that the organizers introduced in 2006. The effort paid off by reducing trash at the festival by about a third; organizers hope to hit the 75 percent mark in trash reduction by 2008. All that while the festival grows annually, adding teams to the competition, vendors to the "Main Street" area, and visitors to the lovely locale.

For more information, go to www.blueridgebbqfestival.com.

Metric Conversion Guide

• •

*N**ote:* The recipes in this cookbook were not developed or tested using metric measures. There may be some variation in quality when converting to metric units.

Common Abbreviations

Abbreviation(s)	What It Stands For
C, c	cup
g	gram
kg	kilogram
L, l	liter
lb	pound
mL, ml	milliliter
oz	ounce
pt	pint
t, tsp	teaspoon
T, TB, Tbl, Tbsp	tablespoon

Volume

U.S. Units	Canadian Metric	Australian Metric
¼ teaspoon	1 mL	1 ml
½ teaspoon	2 mL	2 ml
1 teaspoon	5 mL	5 ml

(continued)

Volume (continued)

U.S. Units	Canadian Metric	Australian Metric
1 tablespoon	15 mL	20 ml
¼ cup	50 mL	60 ml
⅓ cup	75 mL	80 ml
½ cup	125 mL	125 ml
⅔ cup	150 mL	170 ml
¾ cup	175 mL	190 ml
1 cup	250 mL	250 ml
1 quart	1 liter	1 liter
1½ quarts	1.5 liters	1.5 liters
2 quarts	2 liters	2 liters
2½ quarts	2.5 liters	2.5 liters
3 quarts	3 liters	3 liters
4 quarts	4 liters	4 liters

Weight

U.S. Units	Canadian Metric	Australian Metric
1 ounce	30 grams	30 grams
2 ounces	55 grams	60 grams
3 ounces	85 grams	90 grams
4 ounces (¼ pound)	115 grams	125 grams
8 ounces (½ pound)	225 grams	225 grams
16 ounces (1 pound)	455 grams	500 grams
1 pound	455 grams	½ kilogram

Measurements

Inches	Centimeters
½	1.5
1	2.5
2	5.0
3	7.5
4	10.0
5	12.5
6	15.0
7	17.5
8	20.5
9	23.0
10	25.5
11	28.0
12	30.5
13	33.0

Temperature (Degrees)

Fahrenheit	Celsius
32	0
212	100
250	120
275	140
300	150
325	160
350	180

(continued)

Temperature *(continued)*

375	190
400	200
425	220
450	230
475	240
500	260

Index

• T •

BUSINESS, CAREERS & PERSONAL FINANCE

0-7645-9847-3

0-7645-2431-3

Also available:

- Business Plans Kit For Dummies
  0-7645-9794-9
- Economics For Dummies
  0-7645-5726-2
- Grant Writing For Dummies
  0-7645-8416-2
- Home Buying For Dummies
  0-7645-5331-3
- Managing For Dummies
  0-7645-1771-6
- Marketing For Dummies
  0-7645-5600-2

- Personal Finance For Dummies
  0-7645-2590-5*
- Resumes For Dummies
  0-7645-5471-9
- Selling For Dummies 0-7645-5363-1
- Six Sigma For Dummies
  0-7645-6798-5
- Small Business Kit For Dummies
  0-7645-5984-2
- Starting an eBay Business For Dummies
  0-7645-6924-4
- Your Dream Career For Dummies
  0-7645-9795-7

HOME & BUSINESS COMPUTER BASICS

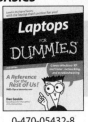

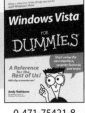

0-470-05432-8

0-471-75421-8

Also available:

- Cleaning Windows Vista
  For Dummies 0-471-78293-9
- Excel 2007 For Dummies
  0-470-03737-7
- Mac OS X Tiger For Dummies
  0-7645-7675-5
- MacBook For Dummies
  0-470-04859-X
- Macs For Dummies 0-470-04849-2
- Office 2007 For Dummies
  0-470-00923-3

- Outlook 2007 For Dummies
  0-470-03830-6
- PCs For Dummies 0-7645-8958-X
- Salesforce.com For Dummies
  0-470-04893-X
- Upgrading & Fixing Laptops For Dummies 0-7645-8959-8
- Word 2007 For Dummies
  0-470-03658-3
- Quicken 2007 For Dummies
  0-470-04600-7

FOOD, HOME, GARDEN, HOBBIES, MUSIC & PETS

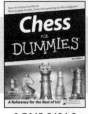

0-7645-8404-9

0-7645-9904-6

Also available:

- Candy Making For Dummies
  0-7645-9734-5
- Card Games For Dummies
  0-7645-9910-0
- Crocheting For Dummies
  0-7645-4151-X
- Dog Training For Dummies
  0-7645-8418-9
- Healthy Carb Cookbook For Dummies 0-7645-8476-6

- Home Maintenance For Dummies
  0-7645-5215-5
- Horses For Dummies 0-7645-9797-3
- Jewelry Making & Beading
  For Dummies 0-7645-2571-9
- Orchids For Dummies 0-7645-6759-4
- Puppies For Dummies 0-7645-5255-4
- Rock Guitar For Dummies
  0-7645-5356-9
- Sewing For Dummies 0-7645-6847-7
- Singing For Dummies 0-7645-2475-5

INTERNET & DIGITAL MEDIA

0-470-04529-9

0-470-04894-8

Also available:

- Blogging For Dummies
  0-471-77084-1
- Digital Photography For Dummies
  0-7645-9802-3
- Digital Photography All-in-One Desk Reference For Dummies
  0-470-03743-1
- Digital SLR Cameras and Photography For Dummies
  0-7645-9803-1
- eBay Business All-in-One Desk Reference For Dummies
  0-7645-8438-3

- HDTV For Dummies
  0-470-09673-X
- Home Entertainment PCs
  For Dummies 0-470-05523-5
- MySpace For Dummies
  0-470-09529-6
- Search Engine Optimization
  For Dummies 0-471-97998-8
- Skype For Dummies 0-470-04891-3
- The Internet For Dummies
  0-7645-8996-2
- Wiring Your Digital Home
  For Dummies 0-471-91830-X

* Separate Canadian edition also available

† Separate U.K. edition also available

Available wherever books are sold. For more information or to order direct: U.S. customers visit www.dummies.com or call 1-877-762-2974.
U.K. customers visit www.wileyeurope.com or call 0800 243407. Canadian customers visit www.wiley.ca or call 1-800-567-4797.

 WILEY

SPORTS, FITNESS, PARENTING, RELIGION & SPIRITUALITY

0-471-76871-5   0-7645-7841-3

Also available:

- Catholicism For Dummies
  0-7645-5391-7
- Exercise Balls For Dummies
  0-7645-5623-1
- Fitness For Dummies 0-7645-7851-0
- Football For Dummies 0-7645-3936-1
- Judaism For Dummies 0-7645-5299-6
- Potty Training For Dummies
  0-7645-5417-4

- Buddhism For Dummies
  0-7645-5359-3
- Pregnancy For Dummies
  0-7645-4483-7 †
- Ten Minute Tone-Ups For Dummies
  0-7645-7207-5
- NASCAR For Dummies 0-7645-7681-X
- Religion For Dummies 0-7645-5264-3
- Soccer For Dummies 0-7645-5229-5
- Women in the Bible For Dummies
  0-7645-8475-8

TRAVEL

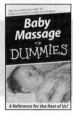

0-7645-7749-2   0-7645-6945-7

Also available:

- Alaska For Dummies 0-7645-7746-8
- Cruise Vacations For Dummies
  0-7645-6941-4
- England For Dummies 0-7645-4276-1
- Europe For Dummies 0-7645-7529-5
- Germany For Dummies
  0-7645-7823-5
- Hawaii For Dummies 0-7645-7402-7

- Italy For Dummies 0-7645-7386-1
- Las Vegas For Dummies
  0-7645-7382-9
- London For Dummies 0-7645-4277-X
- Paris For Dummies 0-7645-7630-5
- RV Vacations For Dummies
  0-7645-4442-X
- Walt Disney World & Orlando
  For Dummies 0-7645-9660-8

GRAPHICS, DESIGN & WEB DEVELOPMENT

0-7645-8815-X   0-7645-9571-7

Also available:

- 3D Game Animation For Dummies
  0-7645-8789-7
- AutoCAD 2006 For Dummies
  0-7645-8925-3
- Building a Web Site For Dummies
  0-7645-7144-3
- Creating Web Pages For Dummies
  0-470-08030-2
- Creating Web Pages All-in-One Desk
  Reference For Dummies
  0-7645-4345-8
- Dreamweaver 8 For Dummies
  0-7645-9649-7

- InDesign CS2 For Dummies
  0-7645-9572-5
- Macromedia Flash 8 For Dummies
  0-7645-9691-8
- Photoshop CS2 and Digital
  Photography For Dummies
  0-7645-9580-6
- Photoshop Elements 4 For Dummies
  0-471-77483-9
- Syndicating Web Sites with RSS Feeds
  For Dummies
  0-7645-8848 6
- Yahoo! SiteBuilder For Dummies
  0-7645-9800-7

NETWORKING, SECURITY, PROGRAMMING & DATABASES

0-7645-7728-X   0-471-74940-0

Also available:

- Access 2007 For Dummies
  0-470-04612-0
- ASP.NET 2 For Dummies
  0-7645-7907-X
- C# 2005 For Dummies
  0-7645-9704-3
- Hacking For Dummies
  0-470-05235-X
- Hacking Wireless Networks
  For Dummies
  0-7645-9730-2
- Java For Dummies
  0-470-08716-1

- Microsoft SQL Server 2005
  For Dummies 0-7645-7755-7
- Networking All-in-One Desk
  Reference For Dummies
  0-7645-9939-9
- Preventing Identity Theft For Dummies
  0-7645-7336-5
- Telecom For Dummies
  0-471-77085-X
- Visual Studio 2005 All-in-One Desk
  Reference For Dummies
  0-7645-9775-2
- XML For Dummies
  0-7645-8845-1

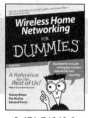

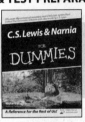

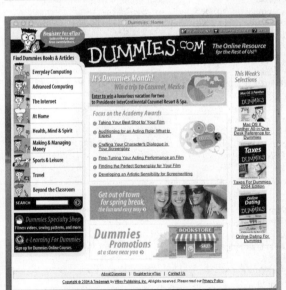